Devotions
for the
Divorcing

William E. Thompson

Foreword by William B. Oglesby, Jr.

John Knox Press
ATLANTA

Library of Congress Cataloging in Publication Data

Thompson, William E., 1936—
    Devotions for the divorcing.

    1. Divorced people—Prayer-books and devotions—
English. I. Title.
BV4596.D58T47   1985   242'.84   85-42827
ISBN 0-8042-2525-7

© copyright John Knox Press 1985
10 9 8 7 6 5 4 3 2 1
Printed in the United States of America
John Knox Press
Atlanta, Georgia 30365

Acknowledgment for permission to reprint is made to the following publishers:

To Charles Scribner's Sons for Ernest Hemingway, excerpt from *A Farewell to Arms*. Copyright 1929 Charles Scribner's Sons; copyright renewed 1957 Ernest Hemingway. Reprinted with the permission of Charles Scribner's Sons.

To Harcourt Brace Jovanovich, Inc. for excerpt from "The Hollow Men" in COLLECTED POEMS 1909–1962 by T.S. Eliot, copyright 1936 by Harcourt Brace Jovanovich, Inc.; copyright © 1963, 1964 by T.S. Eliot. Reprinted by permission of the publisher.

To Harper & Row, Publishers, Inc. for excerpt from "Credo" (p. 743) from YOU CAN'T GO HOME AGAIN by Thomas Wolfe. Copyright, 1934, 1937, 1938, 1939, 1940, by Maxwell Perkins as Executor. Renewed 1968 by Paul Gitlin, Administrator CTA. Reprinted by permission of Harper & Row, Publishers, Inc.

To Macmillan Publishing Company for excerpt from W. B. Yeats, "The Second Coming," *The Poems of W. B. Yeats,* edited by Richard J. Finneran, copyright 1924 by Macmillan Publishing Co., Inc., renewed 1952 by Bertha Georgie Yeats. Reprinted with the permission of Macmillan Publishing Company.

To Westminster Press for words appearing on p. 52 from Hugh T. Kerr, "God of Our Life, Through All the Circling Years," THE CHURCH SCHOOL HYMNAL FOR YOUTH, copyright, 1928; renewed 1956 by Board of Christian Education of the Presbyterian Church in the U.S.A. Used by permission of The Westminster Press.

To the World Student Christian Federation for words from "Thine Is the Glory" by Edmond Budry, from *Cantate Domino.* Copyright World Student Christian Federation. Used by permission.

1583

Appreciation

I wish to thank Dr. William B. Oglesby, Jr., whose ministry and friendship germinated this project, and also his colleague, Dr. William V. Arnold, whose two books, *Divorce: Prevention or Survival* and *When Your Parents Divorce,* were among the first really good materials that I read on this subject. Their counsel and the resources available in the library of their institution, Union Theological Seminary in Virginia, have been most helpful. I also wish to acknowledge the encouragement of a divorced friend, Marge Shaw, who has critiqued this project almost from the beginning. Thanks also to my friends in The Church of the Pilgrims in Washington, D.C., a parish without parallel. Although it is notoriously imperfect at times, it is the best community I can imagine for holding a person together whenever life seems to be coming apart. Its motto is, "Where All Are Pilgrims and No One Is a Stranger." Many a divorcing person has found the reality of this truth while spending part of the journey in that company. I especially thank two Pilgrims: my friend and pastor, Sidney Skirvin, who heard of my unfinished manuscript shortly after we became colleagues in ministry and who has continued in every way to encourage its completion and Patricia Goeldner who helped with the typing at critical points when my church responsibilities and this particular creation were not compatible with one another. In the final analysis this book is about the human/divine glue of faith, hope, and love which prevents people from flying apart in self-destruction or from turning inward in despair and inertia. I want to acknowledge that in so many of the interesting seasons of my own life I have freely received generous amounts of that glue from my dear friends and extended family members, Ray and Bette Wright. I have learned so much from the quality of pastoral care which I have seen and experienced in their lives.

In varying ways all of these people have been biblical "angels," the special messengers of God, who by their voices and touches have often reminded me of the presence of God. Whatever the geography of your journey, I hope you find similar angels along the way.

Foreword

There is pain in divorce, pain that takes many forms and shapes. Sometimes it is guilt, sometimes anger. Helplessness and hopelessness are no strangers to divorcing people. Bewilderment, shame, and yearning tug at the heart and blot out the light. And loneliness, always loneliness. As I prepared to write this Foreword, I read again Thompson's "Pastoral Letter" which introduces the devotions. It is a powerful statement of reality and of hope, and I found myself responding to it again with a sense of gratitude that he is able to state so well the meaning of grace in the presence of despair.

I recall clearly the seminar I had the privilege to conduct for clergy in the Washington, D.C. area on "Pastoral Care and Divorce." Each student was to devise a "term project" that would be useful in meaningful ministry. As would be expected, the papers dealt with a variety of emphases. Willie Thompson prepared "Ten Devotions for the Divorcing." I had not seen anything like that and urged him to expand the number and submit them for publication. Meanwhile, with his permission, I used the devotions in other seminars for pastoral care of divorcing persons. Again and again participants in the seminars affirmed the value of the devotions—an affirmation especially powerful and poignant from those who were, themselves, divorced.

And now the publication is a reality. There is no way of knowing the blessing that the use of these devotions will bring to countless people. Not all divorcing persons will be able to relate to these meditations, prayers, and Scriptures in the same fashion. Even so, I am convinced that there is great power and grace here. Ministers can place the book in the hands of parishioners; families and friends will find new and deeper understanding as they experience the pain of divorce in their loved ones; and, primarily, the persons who no longer can walk together in marriage will discover the power of reconciliation, which binds us all in the family of faith.

I wish, therefore, to thank Willie Thompson for blessing us through these writings, whatever our own isolation or loneliness. And I pray God's blessing on those who will be enriched by these devotions, that they may continue to draw strength from him whose grace is sufficient and whose power is made perfect in our weakness (2 Corinthians 12:9).

—William B. Oglesby, Jr.

Contents

TO MARY

"For there is hope for a tree,
   if it be cut down, that it will sprout again,
   and that its shoots will not cease.
Though its root grow old in the earth,
   and its stump die in the ground,
yet at the scent of water it will bud
   and put forth branches like a young plant."

(Job 14:7–9)

A Pastoral Letter to a Divorcing Friend

My dear friend,

You are not alone. Divorce just makes you *feel* that you are alone. You are afraid, overwhelmed by failure, perhaps angry. Perhaps, also, you feel wretchedly lonely and unworthy. But you are *not* alone. It is natural to feel guilty about failing in one of life's most basic experiences, perhaps even more so if you are a person of faith, properly nurtured and churched since childhood. Sometimes it feels as if this is more than the ending of a relationship; it's almost as if it were the ending of *you*, with all of your relationships and history, memories and hopes. You wish that you could wake up and joyfully discover either that it never happened or that it is all over. With the Psalmist you can truthfully cry:

> *The snares of death encompassed me;*
> *the pangs of Sheol laid hold on me;*
> *I suffered distress and anguish.*
> (Psalm 116:3)

You are not alone. Divorce just makes you *feel* that you are alone. Sometimes good, decent people in your families and churches unwittingly conspire to make you assume that you even *deserve* to be alone, although that is truly a contradiction of the Christian gospel. When I mentioned this devotional project to an Episcopal priest friend of mine, he was mildly shocked, chiding me for sanctioning divorce as a commendable Christian lifestyle. His reaction as a churchman, alas, is not atypical, as you have perhaps discovered. I explained to him, and I will say to you, that, while I still applaud marriage in all of its wonderful dimensions—at best a great mystery, like the relationship of Christ and his church (Ephesians 5:32)—I certainly feel that divorce can *also* be most commendable and, in its own way, graceful (i.e., full of grace).

My priest friend believes marriage to be a sacrament, and since divorce is its antithesis, for him divorce is literally an antichrist force stalking the land. My marriage theology is less sacramental, more pragmatic, and hopefully more pastoral. I believe it is also biblical. *Of course* I honor marriage as the relational ideal for Christians. You and I recognize that to participate in marriage at its best is to experience something very close to godliness.

But such intensity and goodness is rarely sustained in that precise nature. There are very few married persons who have not harbored in their hearts the passing fantasy of chucking it all—the hopes, the ideals, the marriage. In our "out front" age more people are choosing to move from that fantasy to fact. They agree with the apostle that "we all make many mistakes" (James 3:2), and that their marriage has been one of them, regardless of how long or how short it has lasted.

We need to understand that mistakes are simply mistakes; they are not necessarily moral failures, nor should we automatically call every mistake sub-Christian behavior. The Lord Jesus Christ is at home with mistakes. That's why he came and why he suggested frankly that those who were well and healthy did not need the healing he represented. These reasons, also, are why I am so sure that you are not alone.

For some people your separation and divorce will be a surprise, but probably not for as many as you might think. Even if the two of you managed to play the public game rather well, this reality that you now experience certainly did not come as a surprise to *you*. You saw it coming, just as surely as Elijah knew that the "little cloud like a man's hand . . . rising out of the sea" (1 Kings 18:44) was a harbinger of the eventual deluge. Finally there came the moment when both of you admitted, with the Lamenter, "our days were numbered; for our end had come" (Lamentations 4:18).

"Goodness" and Christian pedigree and the accumulated effects of Christian nurture seem to have very little to do with lessening the occurrence of this sociological reality in our day. Certainly the church is no longer the deterrent force that it once was perceived. Indeed, more and more it seems that the daughters and sons of the so-called "pillars of the church" are themselves unable to establish permanent Christian homes. Divorce is happening not only among the offspring of our church mothers and fathers, but also, increasingly, among "pillars" themselves, both laity and clergy. We see many divorces among couples who have been married for decades; who are proven saints, acknowledged and honored church officers; and who are stable members of business and society at large. They include those who have exercised effective church leadership at many levels.

No, divorce is not a respecter of priestly pedigree, prophetic performance, or ecclesiastical involvement. As I see it, this should not astonish the assembled saints. Divorce among the Lord's servants is at least as old as Hosea; and a close, objective reading of the sagas of the patriarchs and matriarchs gives numerous clues that all was not exactly idyllic underneath the tent flaps.

You are not alone. Divorce just makes you *feel* that you are alone. In one respect, however, our generation of divorcing Christians *is* different. Fortunately, many of these essentially good people are *not* tuning out the faith community, nor is the community of faith tuning out the divorcing, as was done by and to your counterparts in previous generations. This is a very important affirmation for everyone. Separation and divorce, in my opinion, offers the faith community one of its *most profound* ways to declare its theology and to express its pastoral care. Too many of our divorcing forebears did not find such experiential love and justice in the faith stance that they and their families took. In short, the church has not always practiced what it preached—the gospel of grace.

I *think* I know what you are feeling. I have found that divorcing Christians, especially in those first weeks and months, are exceedingly skeptical of mother church, as well as their sisters and brothers therein. Almost to a person the principals themselves possess an uncertain theology of divorce. Many of them are totally ignorant of their church's official position on the subject they are experiencing and they make wrong assumptions about what their church thinks. Most of them are quite anxious to know if that fellowship, which they have long treasured and conscientiously served, has any room in its inn for them *still,* now that each, as a "rough beast, its hour come round at last,/Slouches towards Bethlehem to be born" ("The Second Coming," William Butler Yeats). Does the God who established, and blessed as "very good" (Genesis 1:31) that first home in Eden, also stand at the threshold of a broken home that lies somewhere in a wilderness "east of the garden of Eden" (Genesis 3:24)? I believe that God does, and that's why I am sure that you are not alone.

Standing barely inside the door of a broken (breaking) home, you are likely to be so preoccupied with your own dynamics that you are tempted to assume that nearly everything and everyone outside the door is so together that no one there could possibly want you, or have any use for you, since obviously you are anything but together! That's where you are wrong. As Henri Nouwen has so helpfully reminded us, when the Threshold Presence comes to us, knocking, he does not present himself as a "Holy Other" but as our "Wounded Healer," a Friend who bears in his own body *our* marks; but miracle of miracles, we find that it is *with those very marks*, now transformed in him, that we are healed, or saved. The biblical word for "saved" is *soteria*, wholeness, completely put together, a redeemed Humpty Dumpty.

In our Christian theology of grace, it is actually your very *divorce*—not some possible remarriage—that represents a starting all over again. Divorce is not a return to a former state. It is the ending of one condition and the beginning of a new one, then and there! Whoever Jesus Christ is to you, this much is absolutely certain: he is at home with your beginning again. He invited such, saying, "You must be born anew" (John 3:7). Separation is the labor pain of a new life; divorce is its birthing moment. And Jesus Christ is not ashamed to be there. After all Emmanuel (God-Being-Right-There-With-Us) was one of his prophetic names, his essential nature. And that assurance given in the name itself was communicated at a crucial moment (Matthew 1:23), to Joseph *precisely* when he "being a just man and unwilling to put her to shame, (had) resolved to divorce her quietly" (Matthew 1:19) which was the legal way to break a betrothal in his day. I am not sure of all of the theological implications of the fact that Joseph was at the point of divorcing Mary, but I do cite this as further proof that the God who was so intimately involved with these two persons in all of their hopes and fears cannot possibly be withdrawn from you and the awesome fact and the feelings of *divorce*.

You are not alone. Divorce just makes you *feel* that you are alone. If you need any further proof of what I am saying, consider Good Friday, the ultimate form of separation and divorce. "My God, my God, why hast thou forsaken me?" (Mark 15:34). In that awesome moment Jesus was *divorced*, separated out, descended into the hellish nonpresence of the Being with whom he had been completely at one from all eternity. This cry of divorced dereliction is the divorcing

4

person's surest proof of our Savior's understanding, accepting, and suffering love for each and every separated person. Conversely, Easter morning is an alleluia answer that such a divorce was not going to be God's final word. And neither will yours. "Lo, Jesus meets us./Risen from the tomb,/Lovingly He greets us,/Scatters fear and gloom" ("Thine Is the Glory," Edmond Budry). One way of interpreting that great Easter hymn, which we have all sung, is that Jesus also meets us coming out of *our* tombs and greets us, scattering fear and gloom, when we thought we had reached an absolute dead end.

In some parts of our culture this scary new beginning of life happens now to nearly one out of every two couples, who thought that in marrying one another they had already made their one and only new beginning "'til death do us part." You have now become one of those re-beginning statistics, in your conscience and life, and in the life of your family, church, and community. As is true with most of our ambiguous conditions, there are mixed reasons for your being there. The church has often gotten into trouble when it has assumed unto itself the assigning of moral values to those reasons. The church is at its best when it simply stands up for its basic reasons for being—namely, that although you are there in those unpleasant circumstances, you are nevertheless a child of God, one "so loved . . . that he gave his only Son, that whoever believes in him should not perish" (John 3:16). No human mistake can ever undo this which God has done for you. That's why you don't have to be afraid under these circumstances, and again why I am very sure that you are not really alone. Certainly our mistakes have their way of making us feel bad, and hopefully of re-ordering some of our priorities, but it is important to remember that mistakes do not have the power to stay the hand of God's mercy, which always reaches out to me *"just as I am* [married *or* divorced *or* never-married], *without one plea"* ("Just As I Am, Without One Plea," Charlotte Elliott).

We recall that the divorcing Hosea confessed that it was in the very midst of his divorce proceedings that the grace of God healed him, and it was out of that profound experience that he gained his best insight into the nature of this God whom he had long worshiped.

While I do not believe that God sent this divorce upon you through some ecclesiastical fiat, nor by any celestially predestined judgment, I *do* believe that this circumstance has within it the capacity for God's grace and thereby an opportunity for your own Christian growth. Twice in the extant biblical literature the Apostle Paul counseled his colleagues about "making the most of the time" (Ephesians 5:16; Colossians 4:5). True, this *is* a difficult time for you. No one has to confirm that for you. But it is also a time that is capable of being redeemed. You and Emmanuel together can make the most of it, if you so choose. Even the biblical Lamenter in his sorest moments saw as much:

> But this I call to mind,
>   and therefore I have hope:
>
> The steadfast love of the LORD never ceases,
>   his mercies never come to an end;
> they are new every morning;
>   great is thy faithfulness.

(Lamentations 3:21–23)

Koheleth, the nom-de-plume for the preacher-poet of Ecclesiastes, wrote:

> For everything there is a season, and a time for every matter under heaven: . . .
> a time to plant, and a time to pluck up what is planted.

(Ecclesiastes 3:1, 2)

Marriage is the planting season; divorce is the plucking up season. Both are writ large into the essential rhythms of life. Neither is a judgment; both are simply facts of life. Divorce is not all bad. Koheleth also wrote, "Better is the end of a thing than its beginning" (Ecclesiastes 7:8).

Ernest Hemingway has a marvelous commentary on the human condition: "The world breaks every one and afterward many are strong at the broken places" (*A Farewell to Arms,* New York: Charles Scribner's Sons, p. 239, 1929). Not necessarily everyone becomes strong, but many do. And you can be among them, if you allow faith to play a part.

A colleague of mine used to include a reminder in his benedictions: "Remember, nothing is good or bad until God gets through with it." Divorcing Christians, with all of their ambivalent feelings about

6

themselves and about life in general, need to take that reassurance to heart. The only thing that God *ever* pronounced "finished" was his saving work in Jesus Christ (John 19:30). God never implied that he was through with us!

Theologian Paul Tillich had a great sermon entitled "You Are Accepted." That is the essence of our unchanging faith, yesterday, today, and tomorrow, a faith based on what God has done, not on what you have done or not done. And that includes your separation and divorce. No, you are not alone. Divorce just makes you *feel* that you are alone. God is there too.

When I was a child, my minister-father was allowed to perform the wedding ceremony for someone whom the courts had declared to be "the innocent party" in a preceding divorce. What a denial of the gospel! There *are* no innocent parties in the dispensation of God, for "all have sinned and fall short of the glory of God" (Romans 3:23). "None is righteous, no, not one" (Romans 3:10). "Guilt" or "innocence" are not the points of fine distinction for the church. Christ and Christ alone is all that counts.

You can bet your life on that good news. Yes, even your divorcing life! For ". . . to God would I commit my cause; who does great things and unsearchable, marvelous things without number" (Job 5:8, 9). When Paul wrote, "For I am sure that neither . . . things present, nor things to come, nor powers, nor height, nor depth, nor anything else in all creation, will be able to separate us from the love of God in Christ Jesus our Lord" (Romans 8:38, 39), surely a part of the "anything else in all creation" was the possibility of separation and divorce.

The power of these gospel truths does not mean that you will escape stress and distress in these coming days and nights. That's largely because, even though God is perfect, the rest of us are not. That's why, even though our faith tells us that we are *not* alone, we nevertheless often feel that way. The Bible's ultimate person for feeling all alone, beweeping his outcast state and troubling deaf heaven with his bootless cries, while looking upon himself and cursing his fate, was Job. Seemingly, he was divorced by the very deity whom he trusted and served so faithfully. Yet Job left us a beautiful image of hope rising out of his lonely despair:

"For there is hope for a tree,
if it be cut down, that it will sprout again,
and that its shoots will not cease.
Though its root grow old in the earth,
and its stump die in the ground,
yet at the scent of water it will bud
and put forth branches like a young plant."
(Job 14: 7–9)

Whenever you feel that this is you, my friend, just remember the quest of the woman at the well of Sychar, she who was divorced many times over: "Sir, give me this water, that I may not thirst" (John 4:15). "Jesus said to her, 'I who speak to you am he'" (John 4:26).

These devotions are little sips of that water, offered for your refreshment. There are forty of them; there could have been many more. Over the many years that I have been working on these, I have written over twice that number. I finally decided to limit them to forty, because forty is preeminently the Wilderness Number. These devotions are for faith people who find themselves in a wilderness—at times relieved to be removed from their impoverished state of bondage, at times longing for the familiar sights and sounds of Goshen's slavery, folks who are making their vulnerable way through an alien, unfamiliar, and frightening place—one filled with all manner of wildlife and carrion—an environment where there are few signposts, sparse signs of life, and almost no rootage. The wilderness is always a place of surprises and uncertainties, which demand resourcefulness and constant adaptation if the traveler is to survive.

Usually the wilderness people are unable to conjure up sufficient nourishment for themselves. Instead, they survive on manna and water, gifts over which they have no control. Wilderness people know the exhilaration of escape, the uncertain blessings of the law, and their desires to rebel against it. And often there are the hints of an eventual land of promise—somewhere, somehow—if they can just live long enough.

Yes, forty, the Wilderness Number, seemed exactly right. Implicit in this number are all the symbols of grace that God gives in the midst of a journey marked by relief and fear, guilt and anger, despair and hope. Here are the manna and water for nourishment, the pillar of cloud by day and of fire by night for guidance, the covenanting and the law for hope and order, and the portable tabernacle of God's tenting presence, which is your security wherever you wander.

Forty is also the Deluge Number, another suggestive description for this period in many divorced people's lives, when there is no assurance whether you will be drowned in the abyss once "all the fountains of the great deep burst forth" (Genesis 7:11) or whether, as in the Exodus, you will pass over to dry land. Forty is also our Lord's Preparation Number. He moved intentionally from familial life into the abundant dimensions of public ministry, by introspection, fasting, prayer, and temptation. His struggle, like your own, was a struggle with the inner needs of personal hunger, the outer needs of community expectation, and ultimately the deepest needs of finding a life order that makes growth possible.

Wilderness, Deluge, Preparation—a divorcing period is all of these, on different days, in different stages, in one sense or another.

As you move through your own days, naming them for what they are, remember that in every case the Bible testifies that grace abounds for you even in the midst of that uncertain time:

> *He [God] found him in a desert land,*
>   *and in the howling waste of the wilderness;*
> *he encircled him, he cared for him,*
>   *he kept him as the apple of his eye.*
>   (Deuteronomy 32:10)

> *But God remembered Noah and all . . . that were with him in the ark.*
>   (Genesis 8:1)

> *Jesus . . . was led by the Spirit* (Luke 4:1)

> *. . . and the angels ministered to him.* (Mark 1:13)

Beyond the Wilderness came purposeful, rooted living in a land flowing with milk and honey. Beyond the Deluge came the dove bearing the olive branch, followed by the great rainbow of hope. Beyond the Preparation Jesus said, "The time is fulfilled, and the kingdom of God is at hand" (Mark 1:15).

Amen! May it be so, even for you!

Faithfully yours,

A Friend Along the Way

9

1

The New Word for the New Day

"Days of affliction come to meet me."
(Job 30:27)

"Today is the first day of the rest of your life." I wonder who made up that familiar line, and how many times I have heard it? It certainly applies to me today. This is the first day that I have officially had the adjective "divorced" attached to my identity.

Technically, it's "separated" and not "divorced," since we are still in the process, but the emotional impact is the same. When you are divorcing, there are many terms to quibble over, but you can hardly debate this term. Divorce it is: for me and for J. That's a heavy word, one that I will probably have some trouble getting used to hearing and seeing and feeling. It seems so inescapable. From now on, that's a classification word and an experience term that I will simply have to acknowledge as a part of my personal history. Up until yester-day when we physically moved apart and signed some papers, separation/divorce was a pending reality that I could sometimes ignore. But not now. It's there, and I don't suppose that word will ever completely go away after today, no, not even if, eventually, I remarry.

Can a single little word change a whole complex person? Will it make me feel any different, or look any different, or act any different? Hester Prynne in Hawthorne's great novel had her "scarlet letter," *A* for *Adulterer,* emblazoned on her clothing, but the quality of her life was such that eventually that same *A* was engraved upon her tombstone, a mute tribute of silent nobility. Today I feel as if a big *D* for *Divorced* were emblazoned on a sign hung around my neck, the announcement complete with a few flashing lights and a siren. Will time and my own character ever hope to ennoble my psychological stigmata?

Divorced/Separated—that's my word for today; that's me from

this day forward. It feels like a great big moat, isolating me on every side from all the familiar terrain where my life has been heretofore grounded; and I long for the camera tricks of movies and television that show great chasms in the earth miraculously sealing themselves over again. Only in our case I know that would never work.

Loneliness has been a major demon in my life for such a long time; my separation simply institutionalizes it and removes the ambiguity of having to pretend that it is not there. But I know that I don't want to feel as I do today, inhabited by loneliness with despair riding on its shoulder, for the rest of my life.

Prayer

Dear God, I remember that the Bible says that one day is like a thousand years with you, and a thousand years are like one day. As I begin a new part of my life today, can you understand when I tell you that it feels as if this day might be a thousand years long? All those other days out there feel as if they are going to be eternally long and continually lonely too. If you understand this sort of thing, please help me to understand it also; and even when I cannot, let me trust your presence in those days, knowing that nothing, not even this awful, branded letter, can separate me from your love which comes to me in Christ Jesus my Lord. Amen.

2

A Divorce Book

Of making many books there is no end, and much study is a weariness of the flesh.

(Ecclesiastes 12:12)

I am sure that Lee meant well, but I resented it. "I found this new book that's all about how to adjust to separation and divorce, and I thought it might help you to read what an expert on the subject says about what you are going through right now. I glanced through the table of contents, and it looked pretty good to me." I smiled and mumbled a sincere thank-you, without revealing that this was the *third* friend who had given me this same book within the past month.

"It looked pretty good to me." What do these friends know about "goodness" and "badness" in my life right now? Nothing looks especially good about any of this to me, whether in fact, or in feelings, or on paper!

Divorcing people are sitting ducks for their well-meaning friends. More often than not, a gift of this sort comes off as a patronizing gesture instead of the caring symbol someone intended. I would much rather experience their continuing friendship than to have the gesture of a printed page. Besides, nobody is "expert" enough to tell me how to feel my way through this coming apart process. I don't care if 99 and 44/100% of *all* persons feel and act thus-and-so, *I* still have the right to be my own 56/100 without some expert advising me that I am out of step with everyone else!

There are certainly a lot of divorce books on the market, and the truth is that I had glanced through most of them even before we ever separated. I guess I was curious about what to expect. Maybe I even thought that if I could vicariously experience a separation through reading, I might not have to experience the real feeling in the event. But reading is never a substitute for living out a real situation, and we should not try to escape into making it such. Everyone writes her or his own book, copyrighted by each unique set of emotions and experiences. I have no earthly idea what mine will be—how many chapters, how "dirty," how exciting, how boring, how ill-organized. Maybe I should not toss out these giftbooks. They might provide checkpoints for me, lest my own life-book starts turning out useless.

Prayer

O God, you are the only true expert in this business of living and loving. Because you are the authority in all relationships, you came here in the flesh, to share and to show. And that's why you left us your spirit, your special presence (presents?) in our relationships. Amid all the "friendly advice" and "expert opinions" I am hearing these days, help me to turn to you more often, for you have always made yourself at home in the middle of our confusion and uncertainties. If I can just be sure that you and I are writing my story together, I know it will be okay. But what about J.? I pray that you will help J. write a good story too, even if it no longer is one that I share. Amen.

3

Aunt Julia

*"All my intimate friends abhor me,
and those whom I loved have turned against me."*
(Job 19:19)

Today I finally went to see Aunt Julia. It was one of those things I knew I had to do, and I had postponed it for as long as possible. Once I was finally on the way I could hardly wait to get it over with.

Nearly every family has an Aunt Julia. In ours she's Dad's older, unmarried sister, the self-assigned matriarch of that part of our family, the custodian of the family traditions, memories, genealogical records, etc. (How is a divorce noted on one of those family-tree charts? I wondered). I already knew her bottom-line judgment: "We've never had a divorce in our family, you know!"

Should I remind her of their Aunt Marjorie, whose husband simply walked away one day and never came back? All we ever knew was that he was "out West" somewhere. That generation, however, could never make the collective family judgment to suggest that Aunt Marjorie get a divorce. Instead, all of them protected their inviolable family honor. Am I less honorable in my generation than they were in theirs?

I was right about Aunt Julia. After a few incidental words, she bored right in. "Well! You've certainly dropped a thunderbolt into our midst. We've never had a divorce in our family, you know!"

"I know. I'm sorry, Aunt Julia, but maybe our family has never had a couple as mixed up and as hurting as we have been."

Her answer was immediate: "I don't believe that for one minute. People these days just don't want to make the effort to work things out."

I had earlier decided that I would not argue with her. Aunt Julia is

14

angry and hurt and confused, just like I am—only she has nowhere to vent those feelings. My aloneness probably touches a sensitive nerve she's lived with all her life, covering up that isolation by assuming our family mantle.

I have done my duty. I let Aunt Julia tell me how much I have let her down, along with letting down everybody else in our family. I wonder if she will ever understand that I felt that already, even without her pronouncements. I won't try to win her over. She may simply have to live with this and remain angry at me.

But she may not. She looked like she was about to cry when I left her. I certainly was. In fact I did, but not where Aunt Julia would see me. If I had it do to over again, I think I would let her see me. Then she might let me see something more of her, too.

Prayer

Dear Father, how did you feel when Adam and Eve let you down? When Jacob lied? When David committed adultery? Your family honor has been broken so many times. Isn't that what "the fall" is all about? Doesn't "original sin" mean that absolutely everyone in your family eventually lets you down, save Jesus alone? Thank you for sticking by us even when we don't keep your image perfectly. And bless Aunt Julia, for she hurts too. Amen.

4

Mistaken Mail

"This at last is bone of my bones
and flesh of my flesh."
(Genesis 2:23)

Some computerized firm sent a letter to my residence, addressed "Mr. and Mrs." Mr. and Mrs., indeed! That's a nonentity. No wonder they call it junk mail!

Our "and" is gone. We're no longer a conjunctive unit (conjunctive . . . conjugal . . . conjecture!). Maybe we *never* were, and we simply took a long time to admit it. If I remember my grammar correctly, "and" is a correlative conjunction appropriately joining two equals. Two equals? Hah! That was never our marriage!

Strange how an insignificant piece of mail has set me off on such a flight of philosophical fantasy! J. and I weren't much of an "and," yet for a while every civil, ecclesiastical, and social part of our culture said that we were. Who was lying? And who was being lied to? As long as we went along with being "Mr. and Mrs." out front, a lot of things seemed much simpler, even if they weren't that way on the inside.

Do I throw away this mechanically produced letter in the manner some folks say we have thrown away our marriage? Which was the truly mechanical production? The letter or our marriage? Maybe I should return it, marked, "Doesn't live here anymore." That would be true. "Mr. and Mrs." is no longer a unit that lives here. Perversely, there is an impish part of me that wants to write "*Never* lived here." The accurate inscription might be, "Moved, left no forwarding address." We're each heading somewhere else with our lives, and right now neither one of us has any idea about the destination. Someday both J. and I will each have a new forwarding address, a new place where we are truly "at home." But not now.

The poet who saw sermons in every stone doesn't have anything on me! I'm reading my divorce into nearly every item, event, person, word, memory that comes along these days and nights. I'll be so glad when (if?) I ever get beyond this adjustment stage. I guess that divorcing has its growing pains in the same way that adolescence does, or that marriages should.

Prayer

Lord, will the reminders of connectedness ever completely go away? I hope so. This sort of thing could drive me crazy if I allow it. Help me to loosen up a little. Surely not everything that happens is sent by your providence to tell me something about my divorce. Some mail is simply mail; much conversation is just talk; not everyone's plans that affect me have a hidden agenda, just to get some point across. You have promised to make all things new. That must mean that you don't go around playing the same old record all the time, either. Amen.

5

Attending Church

". . . I stood in great fear of the multitude, and the contempt of families terrified me."

(Job 31:34)

"I stand up in the assembly, and cry for help."
(Job 30:28)

I had an uncomfortable experience yesterday.

I was determined to go back to church for the first time since our separation, even though I had been afraid that I would be uncomfortable in church. I remembered that when I was a child I once heard my mother whisper to a friend sitting next to her in church, "Look at *that*, would you? Susan Lamn is back in church. . . . Well, at least she's on the *back* row!" Afterwards I learned that whatever caused Mrs. Lamn's presence to be so noteworthy to Mother—and it was definitely a presence that was supposed to be self-limiting—was something called "a divorce."

That memory, with all the confirming judgments of Mother's friends, came surging to the fore in the weeks while I thought about resuming my church attendance. I debated: maybe I shouldn't have stopped in the first place, not even for one Sunday. Temporarily dropping out may have been a mistake, for that may look like I have been waiting for the judgments to form. But that business about Susan Lamn was many years ago—in fact, over twenty-five years. A quarter of a century. Ancient history. Lots of time and changes since then.

At least I hope so.

Actually, the *going* back to church wasn't bad at all. If there were any gossiping wigwags in my direction, I missed them; but you can be sure that I allowed every affirming smile and nod and embrace, the spoken words and the silent, solid assurances alike, to bathe me thoroughly, body and soul.

The only brief difficulty was one I had not especially thought about beforehand. It caught me offguard. Where would I sit? Like most couples, we had our favorite spot, which all the ushers knew. Thus, when I walked into the narthex, Helen asked, "The usual place?" I nodded and followed her up the aisle. Suddenly I panicked. What if J. were sitting there? After all, J. is still a church member and has every right to be there too. With a relieved sigh, I saw that the place was empty. I sat down. I had not been there two minutes before I knew that "our pew" really *was* empty. It wasn't the same; I couldn't worship at the same place where *we* had worshiped. Should I move elsewhere during the first hymn? No, that would simply advertise my discomfort and my mistaken judgment. Although I've got a right to be uncomfortable, there are some things I have to learn by living through them. Since I had not thought this one through beforehand, I decided to stay put. No use imposing my learning and discomfort on everyone else. But next Sunday, I will sit on the other side.

Prayer

O God, there are some places where I can't be anymore, or where I maybe shouldn't be. But I rejoice to know that you are everywhere, and that helps. I'm glad you aren't fixed to special places, and that your spirit can constantly come to me wherever I am. I *need* a God with that kind of mobility and adaptability. Thank you. Amen.

6

Feeling Guilty

. . . pardon my guilt, for it is great.
(Psalm 25:11)

It's all my fault!

In my saner moments, I know it isn't, but that's not the way I feel today! It doesn't seem to take much to send me off on that familiar guilt trip. Although I used to think that J. went out of the way to lay that one on me, for the most part I am reacting to chance remarks that probably were not intended to load up on me at all. Some of the ones that I recall lately have been:

"You could have knocked me over with a feather when I heard that the two of you . . . "

"I couldn't believe it. I still can't. What happened? We all thought that you were the perfect couple."

"Gee, I've always thought that J. was one of the nicest persons I've ever met."

"I can't tell you how sorry I am. It just makes me sick at my stomach."

"It was the main topic of conversation at the McNeill's dinner party last weekend. I'll have to tell you, it really put a damper on things."

"I'll bet it just *killed* your parents, didn't it?"

"I was just asking Gene, if church couples can't stay together, then who can? What's the world coming to?"

Who made me Atlas, that I have to bear all of this on my shoulders? *I'm* to blame for their lack of equilibrium? *I* call into question their capacity to judge "perfect" couples? What I've done means that J. suddenly is not really a nice person after all? Who made me the caretaker of my parents' very lives? someone else's digestive system? the mood of a dinner party? The reputation of church-related couples? And those are just samples of the kinds of discomforts I am causing others.

Then there's the whole other kind of guilt that I feel because of what this has done to J.—economically, emotionally, spiritually. And who knows! Maybe the worst is yet to come. Have I been too hasty? Have we really thought this through enough? At the same time, *sometimes* I feel guilty that we didn't go ahead and do this a long time ago.

And what about the guilt I bear for what I have done to me? My work performance has suffered to the point that I had to be called in to my supervisor for a conference. Bad as it is now, is it possible that I will be even worse six months from now? How long will I go on feeling like a failure with a big F branded into the middle of my forehead? Will I ever be able to give and to receive and to trust again? What have I done to myself?

Prayer

Lord, do give me a decent sense of perspective. Some of this is *my* fault; most of it is *our* fault. I've read that some of us assume our loads of guilt as a perverted form of pride. Am I guilty of proudly wanting to be the guilty one here? You've promised to remove our guilt and remember our sins no more. I want to trust that promise, just as I am, without challenging you, without pitting my guilt against your grace. You've already loved me, and not because I pushed you. Amen.

7

Violence

A [person] without self-control
is like a city broken into and left without walls.
(Proverbs 25:28)

The newspaper article riveted my attention and stirred my emotions:

Family Shootout Leaves 4 Dead

Pittsburgh, Pa.—A "family council" erupted into a shootout Thursday night. Four people were killed and one wounded. A police spokesperson said that the police were still trying to piece together the sequence of events that led up to the deaths of a couple contemplating divorce and two of the woman's relatives.

That's the sort of report that leaves me shaking a bit, for I remember how strong our own emotions were on occasions during the conflictual time before our separation. Many was the time we almost came to blows; and one awful Wednesday night, we did, although we were both horrified immediately afterwards and were surprised that we both could be genuinely sorry about physically hurting someone when each of us realized we were psychologically hurting one another all the time. How many times did I momentarily have a death wish for J.? What would have happened if I had owned a gun right then? And how about the evening Uncle Jerry came by and said he understood that we had been having trouble, and he wondered if he could do anything to help. That much was okay, if he had just left it at that. The only trouble was that Uncle Jerry proceeded, nonstop for twenty minutes, to tell us how to straighten everything out. When he finally left, J. burst out, "I could strangle him!" I agreed. Both of us were seething. Together. Not at each other as we often were, but at someone else. When a marriage is coming apart, life within it can be like a pressure cooker. The really frightening thing is not being sure where the safety valve is located.

Prayer

O God of peace, there have been so many times lately that the intensity of my feelings surprises—and scares—me. Is this the real me? What is happening to me? Am I going to be this way from now on? I never used to react this way. Maybe the fact that I never used to is a clue that all along I was keeping too much bottled up inside. If both of us had dealt with our little feelings before they became big feelings, maybe we wouldn't be where we are today. At any rate, thank you for helping the two of us deal with our big feelings before they got totally out of control and as destructive as the ones in the news story. And please, O God, bring peace and healing to those who remain in that Pittsburgh family. And in ours. Amen.

8

Tears

*"My face is red with weeping,
and on my eyelids is deep darkness."*
(Job 16:16)

Last night I wept. There was no obvious precipitating cause, absolutely no rhyme nor reason. It caught me by surprise while I was out shopping. I don't cry easily, and I am certainly not given to crying in public.

I came straight home. There I sobbed—gushing tears that just wouldn't quit. Rage. Bitterness. Resentment. Self-pity. Sadness. Relief. A little bit of each, I guess. It's hay fever season, but that certainly had nothing to do with it. However, I will use that as my public excuse since I'm still sniffly and puffy today.

I've heard all the catch "explanatory" phrases for what was happening to me: "emotional disengagement," "grief work." And of course I have often read of divorce being analogous to death. Yet the death of our relationship lacks a societal and ecclesiastical ritual of passage, where some dynamics can be acted out on cue. Like my crying last night.

So many folks want me to be relieved and happy (so they can be?). "Now that things are settled?" These must be the kind of folks the Bible calls "the foolish . . . and slow of heart." Will those things they refer to ever be settled? I can't pretend away my past with its guilts and regrets—and its goodness. Some things are worth crying about! Tears and anguish feel closer to my real being right now than I can bear.

Will nobody let me cry? Christ suggested that we sometimes ought to go into the closet and pray. Do I have to go into the closet also to cry? Last night I couldn't pray. I could only cry. Perhaps I can pray again someday, but for sure I could cry again *every* day.

Some writers have likened the kind of tears I shed to the evidence of a surgical procedure. Sorrowing helps open up some of the old wounds, so that they can be healed up from within. And crying lets you know they are open. Sealing those wounds over without tears would be to treat the cruel cuts as if they did not really exist. But all the while an ugly scar might be forming on the outside, allowing poisons to be multiplying and heating up on the inside. Both the scar and the fester are likely to cause more problems in the future.

So, come sweet, hot, salty, flowing tears. I do not yet welcome you as I may some day. Right now I find you absolutely overwhelming, but I want to trust what you are doing within me.

Prayer

Jesus, you wept—for Lazarus, for unrepentant Jerusalem. Do you weep for me? How about *with* me? Can you help me to get used to weeping? The Psalmist said that "weeping may tarry for the night, but joy comes with the morning." I'm glad that person also said that you neither slumber nor sleep; I hope that means you will be right here beside me all through these nighttimes of weeping. Even when I don't understand myself and can't seem to control myself, you understand me, and you control me, and you sustain me. And you love me, tears and all. Thank you for your love that cries *with* me. I wonder how J. is handling tears. I don't want J. to cry without remembering your presence there too. Amen.

9

The Radio Preacher

"Shall windy words have an end?"
(Job 16:3)

Driving home from work yesterday, I was listening to one of those preachers talking to all of us who live "out there in radioland." The minute he started haranguing about family life, I should have switched stations; but for some reason I did not. Is that the masochist in me? Sure enough, he started in on "the terrible sin of our high divorce rate" and how *my* kind of statistic (is *this* my ultimate condemnation, to be a statistic?) is "one more evidence of God's judgment on our country."

I don't like people using me to prove their points; I especially don't want church people using my painful situation as an illustration for their theology and for their opinions. As I quickly switched stations, I found myself hoping that the preacher would find out he had a pregnant teenage daughter! Some religious people seem to bring out the worst in me these days.

Maybe I'm too sensitive, but I am continually bothered by how many church folks categorize divorce as a sin. While I'm certainly not proud of our separation, I am quite aware that there was an awful lot of sin there *before* we finally started resolving our connections with a legal separation. And *where* are the preachers with their gospel words against all the gossip, criticism, censure, and ostracism we have both encountered from some parts of society *since* our separation? I don't expect approval, or even sanction, from the religious establishment, but don't I have a right to expect some degree of understanding love? Even amidst the unpleasant reality of my divorce, I would expect somebody in the church to understand that there can surely be a note of justice and peaceful resolution in this process. Wouldn't that be a godly thing?

Religious folks don't make a helpful contribution to my life right now by reminding me of the sacredness of marriage vows, or by telling me how far short I have fallen from the glory of God and God's will. I already know that better than they.

Prayer

Dear God, I don't want to try to pretend that our separation is an ideal event. I wouldn't wish it on any other couple I know. I believe that permanent marriage is still the ideal for all adult Christian relationships. Yet divorce is putting me in the far country, under the judgment of a number of your well-meaning people of the faith. But even you (especially you) called back a redeemed remnant from their Babylonian exile. Will your church let me come back in that same way, as your cleansed, renewed servant, albeit a remnant of who I once was? I hope so. Amen.

10

Our Wedding Anniversary

How the gold has grown dim, how the pure gold is changed!
(Lamentations 4:1)

The joy of our hearts has ceased.
(Lamentations 5:15)

Today is our wedding anniversary. Does it still count? I guess so. After all, our divorce isn't final yet. I know it's a date which no longer deserves a celebration, but should I at least acknowledge the anniversary in a conversation with J.? Probably not. If J. is hurting, it won't accomplish anything to mention the date, and if J. pretends to have forgotten all about it, I'll just be hurt all over again myself.

Widows and widowers can put flowers on the graves of their loved ones on their wedding anniversary dates. But our marriage isn't conveniently laid to rest in a pretty cemetery. It's being laid to rest in lawyers' files, in a courtroom, with a judge's gavel, and with the expenditure of a lot of money. Where, and how, shall we bury the remains? In our check stubs?

"This is the way the world ends/Not with a bang but a whimper." Was T.S. Eliot thinking of a divorce when he wrote those words ("The Hollow Men," ll. 97–98)? We began our life together with a bang, a blow-out. And now we limp along more or less separately until some final whimper.

On our wedding day I really did think it was "the first day of the rest of [my] life." Instead, it worked out to be the first day of the *test* of my life! Finally, we've both had to acknowledge that we've failed the test. Now, so soon after that acknowledgment, this date comes around like a sick joke, only nobody is laughing.

Prayer

Lord, what do you do with your painful anniversaries, Maundy Thursday and Good Friday? You've transformed them into something other than simply a commemoration of agony and disappointment. Is there some way I can do the same with this date? Your sad dates become glad dates through the presence of the community of faith gathered around. Is this a clue for my handling of this same date the next time it comes around? Amen.

11

The Silent Treatment

"They are discomfited, they answer no more;
they have not a word to say.
And shall I wait, because they do not speak,
because they stand there, and answer no more?"
(Job 32:15, 16)

"Behold, I waited for your words."
(Job 32:11)

Today I unexpectedly bumped into Pat during my lunchtime. While we haven't been the best of friends, we certainly have been far more than casual acquaintances. I know that aside from our circle of mutual friends, Pat has certainly had many opportunities to have heard about our separation and has probably discussed it with some of our mutual friends. Yet today Pat never acknowledged my reality anywhere in our exchange of a dozen bits of dialogue. I really would not have cared *which* variation Pat had chosen: "I was really sorry. . . ," or "I was surprised to hear . . . ," or "I frankly am glad that you finally. . . ." The point is that this friend *should* have said something that was real to me, about me.

You can't pretend that something doesn't exist, simply because it is unpleasant to look at or uncomfortable to talk about. Being silent won't make it go away. Pat's avoidance reminds me of the old philosophical question: when a tree falls in the forest and there's no one there to hear it, does it make a noise? My divorce is making plenty of noise to me. I want my friends to admit that they hear it, even if they don't quite know the meaning of the sound. I don't know if it's a "good" sound or a "bad" sound, either. I think a lot of both. The point is that I don't want to have to listen to it all by myself.

I'm being too hard on Pat. Perhaps I need to accept the fact that J.

and I are now embarrassments to some of our friends, for a multitude of reasons, some of which are entirely beyond our control or theirs. The truth is that, even if this friend had tried to say something, I might have considered the results inane or inappropriate. Maybe not.

I'm still me, even in the midst of our separation. I don't want folks to pretend not to see me, "warts and all." After all I'm not a totally transparent person. I resent their looking right through me, ignoring the big gut-level reality that is squarely within me right now.

Prayer

God, the Bible calls you "the Word." I understand that better now than ever before. I think it means that it is your nature to keep on positively communicating through the abyss, to the depths of my real person. Right now a lot of folks are avoiding the pain and ambiguity of giving me "a word." I am grateful that you are always in touch with my real world. Amen.

12

The Emergency Telephone Call

Let not the flood sweep over me,
or the deep swallow me up,
or the pit close its mouth over me.
(Psalm 69:15)

The bedside phone woke me at 1:15 a.m. I was asleep, although just barely, because I had been reading until about 1:00. It was my sister. "Mother seems to have had a slight stroke. It just happened a couple of hours ago. I'm here at the hospital with Daddy. The doctors are still examining her. We aren't sure · how bad it is. She isn't responding to anyone yet, but some of that may be due to the medication they've given her."

I was wide awake now, my adrenalin pouring. I had a dozen questions, but I asked the most important one first. "Can I speak to Dad?"

"Just a minute, I'll see."

After a pause, his familiar voice came on the line, but without its accustomed warmth and strength. "Can you come quickly? I really need you." Then his voice broke, and he cried softly.

Sis came back on. "Are you there?"

"Yes," I replied, "but I'm leaving immediately. I'll be there with you just as soon as I can. Which hospital are you in?"

I jumped up and pulled down my suitcase from the closet shelf and hastily sorted through some items in my dresser. Wait a minute, first I'd better call the airlines. But how can I make airline arrangements, pack my suitcase, cancel tomorrow's appointments, and go to the bathroom, all at the same time, and all by myself?

I almost called J., simply because I was so scared, and it's awful to be scared by yourself. Scared that Mother would die before I could get there, or even *after* I got there. Besides, J. loves my parents too.

What *is* J.'s relationship to my family crisis? Legally we are still married, but emotionally we are separating and physically we are now living apart. Does that mean that J. is divorcing my family too? Would *I* want to know in the middle of the night that one of my erstwhile in-laws was critically ill? Should I call? By J.'s normal getting-up time I will, I hope, be en route. Yet, if I do call, what if J. is in one of those unpredictable moods? The last thing I want to hear is "I'm really sorry, but what do you expect *me* to do about it?" Do I dare ask J. for a ride to the airport? And what happens if Mom dies? Do I expect J. to come?

Prayer

Dear Lord, God of Abraham and Sarah, Isaac and Rebecca, Jacob and Leah and Rachel, I thank you for my parents and for all that they have given me. I want them to be a part of my life as long as possible. Even my broken life. I'm confused about what to expect of J. right now, or what my family may expect, or for that matter what J. wants to give. It's scary to face a family crisis without someone to share your feelings, and it's a little confusing to know who really is "family" right now. At least I know that you are here. Thank you for one certainty among all my uncertainties. Amen.

13

A Funeral

"I have become an alien in their eyes."
(Job 19:15)

Bruce died earlier this week. It wasn't exactly unexpected. He had brain cancer. He and Frances had been especially close to us when we first joined the church. They were the ones who came around to see us after we had signed the visitors' register. In fact I saw J. briefly there at the funeral home, which didn't surprise me; nor did it especially bother me, for J. and Bruce had served on the Worship Committee together for several years. Bruce and Frances, however, never came to see either one of us nor communicated in any kind of way when J. and I separated. But since Bruce already was pretty far along with his cancer, I never really expected to hear from them. I figured they were too busy with their troubles to get involved in ours.

It was a little awkward when Frances first spoke to me in the parlor. She was making a valiant effort to be her typically gracious self. "Oh, there you are! I'm so glad to see you. I was just talking to J. a few minutes ago, and we were remembering that evening when Bruce and I"—I saw the light snap on in her eyes: something that she evidently had not remembered when talking to J. —"well, what I mean is . . . oh, I'm sorry. That's not what I meant to say!" After a few reassurances from me, we hugged and she moved off, probably relieved that there was some other consoler nearby to whom she could speak. I milled around a little, as one does under such circumstances, and a few minutes later I saw Frances looking at me from the sofa where she was now seated. She was looking a hole through me. I figured that right then she probably resented my being alive. And J.'s being alive too. After all, we had deliberately chosen to cut off our relationship with one another, while death, which was beyond their control, had severed her relationship with Bruce. His death was truly an untimely one, for he had been a wonderful man in the full strength of his personal, family, and professional years. Furthermore it looked as if Bruce and Frances had a really good marriage. They had it all together; they were the type of folks you could imagine living happily ever after. Only now they would not. And we could have, but did not.

Prayer

Dear God, if I made Frances uncomfortable, I'm sorry. All I wanted to do was to let her know that I cared for her and for her husband. Maybe she doesn't really resent our separation, although I think she has a right to feel that way. Help her deal with both her discomforts and mine when I am around her family that has been broken by death—J.'s and mine has been broken by something far less devastating in the long run. But, in a way, Frances is fortunate. At least she has an acceptable way for folks to tell her they are sorry, and she has an official religious ritual in which she can begin to have peace. What do you and the fellowship of faith offer J. and me? Amen.

14

The Promotion

"Behold, my heart is like wine that has no vent;
like new wineskins, it is ready to burst."
(Job 32:19)

I'm going to get a promotion and a salary raise! Whenever that happened to either one of us, J. and I used to go out on the town dining and dancing. It was always an occasion for real celebration, whether we could afford it or not.

But this time I don't have anybody to share my good news with. I didn't have anybody to celebrate my birthday with either, but at least then I got several cards from my family members, along with a present from my parents. But my promotion is another kind of event. I received a major commendation, and the company is rewarding me. Back when I was called into the supervisor because my work had suffered, I would not have given a nickel for my chances of achieving this promotion.

It is really something to feel good about—and *I do*—but whom do I have to feel it *with* me, *for* me, *about* me? Nobody. How can I humbly call up someone, explaining what a great person I am? I suppose I could call my parents to tell them all about it again, but it feels as if that would be a child seeking parental approval, and that's not how I want to come through.

J. would probably be genuinely glad for me if I shared that news, but why should I? How long will I go on being beholden to J.'s approval? This is as good a time as any to stop. Besides, I might as well keep this under wraps, since a change in my income might affect our final settlement. No use telling any more than I have to.

Yet, a promotion is a tremendous personal affirmation. I would like to share it with someone special. I wonder if my minister would understand the meaning of this event at this particular time in my life? Probably he would make some inane remark about increasing my financial pledge!

What can I do with my good news?

Prayer

Lord, you really are the good news (*good spiel,* gospel), which carries with it the compulsion to "go tell it on the mountain, over the hills, and everywhere." Good news of every sort ought to be shared. That's a part of the meaning of evangelism (*evangelion,* a good announcement). We Christians are supposed to be your heralds of good tidings. Now I think I understand how frustrating it must be to you when nobody tells your good news around either. Amen.

15

Taking Sides

"My kinsfolk and my close friends have failed me."
(Job 19:14)

Today I was having a Big Mac when Chris came in and came over and ate with me. I have always liked Chris; in fact you could make a case for saying I like Chris better than almost anyone I currently know. But not today. Chris started in, commiserating about our separation, and really wouldn't let up. The most embarrassing and discomforting thing was that Chris was all one-sided, assuming, I guess, that this kind of display would be an affirmation of support and friendship.

Even I am not always on "my" side when I think about our divorce! Why do people assume there are well defined sides? And what gives them the right to self-select their allegiance? I am really disappointed in Chris. Because Chris is J.'s friend too. Or was. Was Chris being honest? Has our separation made Chris select-out my partner? If this is so, will J. think that I influenced Chris?

In separations and divorces there are never any "innocent" parties, and few black-and-white issues. It's not clear to me that there's any particular side to be on. I resent my close friends and folks from my side of the family thinking that I am expecting their absolute, unmitigated loyalty, or more to the point, that I expect it at J.'s expense. We both need and want beholding love, not blind loyalty (I like that: beholding love—a love that is not afraid to see, and a love committed to holding both of us.

Prayer

God, you hold both J. and me like that, and that's wonderful. We sing about Christ's being "the right man on our side." And I'm counting on it. Help J. to recognize this truth too, and to depend on your presence being there. You're on everyone's side. Forgive me whenever I try to make you, or any of my friends, to see things my way. And someday maybe J. and I will be able, with your help, to stop assuming that each of us ever had exclusive ownership of a "right side" either. Amen.

16

No Backup

I sink in deep mire,
where there is no foothold;
I have come into deep waters,
and the flood sweeps over me.
(Psalm 69:2)

The refrigerator repair person is coming tomorrow morning, and I will have to take off from work in order to be there. Two weeks ago it was the electrician and my recurring problem with blown fuses. I don't suppose that there are any more of these problems than there used to be; it's just that we used to switch off with one another on such logistical needs, taking turns on problems we had with what we owned in common, or what we mutually needed, such as the time when J. straightened out our foul-up with the Internal Revenue Service, or when I took care of getting our new car registered when we had both procrastinated until that last snowy day.

There's no backup person in my household right now, and not only is that very inconvenient, it's quite costly as well. Taking off today means that I won't be able to stretch out the next holiday weekend one day longer. And that, in turn, means that I may not get to the family reunion; and, believe it or not, *that* in turn may mean that I lose out on Uncle Bob's will, because I'm not too sure how my divorce sits with the crotchety old man, and I might need to be present at the reunion, just to shore up my inheritance possibilities. "For want of a nail the shoe was lost . . . " (Benjamin Franklin). For want of some refrigerator freon, an inheritance was lost? It doesn't sound very poetic, but who knows? It could be true!

That's not the main problem, of course. If need be, I could probably find a retired neighbor to sit at home until the repair person comes; they've even got businesses now that provide bonded people to do this for an hourly *fee*. The real problem, of course, is that I don't have any *emotional* backup person either, and *that* can be devastating. The absence of, and search for, such a person typically begins long before an acknowledged marital breakup. In fact, I suppose that is more often a cause of infidelity than lust, or curiosity, or the need for adventure.

I need a companion in my life, both to back me up and to be with me. It costs me a lot to have a go at life all alone.

Prayer

Emmanuel, God-with-us, you are in both the companionship business and the backup posture. You refuse to leave us copeless. You counseled, "Comfort ye, comfort ye, . . . speak tenderly . . . and cry unto her that her warfare is accomplished. . . ." In the absence of my having anyone else who can regularly be that to me, and say that to me, I am grateful for your presence. It won't repair a refrigerator or wait for the plumber, but it can do an even greater miracle: it can mend a broken spirit. You are more than a foothold; you are the rock I find in the middle of my muck. Thank you. Amen.

17

Communion

"For I am filled with disgrace . . . "
(Job 10:15)

. . . yet mercy triumphs over judgment.
(James 2:13)

Last Sunday was the first time I had taken communion since we separated. It wasn't that I had turned it down; I just hadn't had the opportunity. The previous "Communion Sunday" in our church I had been sick, so this was my first time.

When I was growing up, I once heard my home church pastor say that he did not think a particular divorced woman should take communion. Informally, and without due process he thus excommunicated her, and I suspect that he treated her that way in other areas of her life. As a child I remember hearing of several divorced people who attended worship services, but would not take communion because they felt "unworthy."

I've never understood that kind of thinking. Who is ever worthy of the sacrament, which represents Christ's broken body and shed blood? Never once in my life have I ever been worthy by virtue of my own strength or merit. I wasn't worthy of sharing in that sacrament when I made my initial profession of faith, or when I attended on a "spiritual high" on Easter morning, or when as a teenager I had been parked by the city lake with the preacher's not-so-saintly kid the night before, or when I took communion once with a hangover, or when J. and I had our first communion after marriage. How was this service on last Sunday any different from the others?

It wasn't that I felt any more sinful last Sunday, or any more out of touch with God than in previous services. If anything, I may have appreciated the service even more than before. "Communion" by its very title means that you are connected: a part of the real presence of our Savior inside of you; a part of the whole company of believers there in the place (the sacrament isn't a private rite; it is a communal celebration); indeed, as The Apostles' Creed says, "the communion of the saints"—my sacramental connection with the company of believers beyond the grave.

Since divorce is a disconnecting event, communion is a kind of spiritual antithesis to what I've been going through. I'm glad that my church does not refuse me this connecting symbol. It's my birthright. In my opinion, only a fool, or a misguided religionist, would pass it up. My communion experience was exactly what I needed.

Prayer

Gracious Lord, I thank you for loving me "just as I am." In my disconnected world I am especially grateful for this opportunity to tune you in—and to be tuned in by you. I like the reminder, "This do in remembrance of me." I need to remember somebody other than myself. I guess that divorcing people think the whole world revolves around them. Help all of us to remember that it still revolves around you. Amen.

18

Needing Advice from My Ex

"I must appeal for mercy to my accuser."
(Job 9:15)

Let not the flood sweep over me,
  or the deep swallow me up,
  or the pit close its mouth over me.
(Psalm 69:15)

Income tax season is worse this year than ever. There are some things that I simply must check out with J. We tried to do it several times over the telephone, but this is simply one of those complicated things that has to be done in person.

I'm going over there tonight, because most of the records are there. Twice before I had made an appointment to do this, but both times I broke it, for what I thought were good and honest reasons. But today is Thursday, April 12th. Time is running out. I'm to be there at 8:00. With luck I'll be out of there before midnight. I wouldn't want to be working with my ex-spouse on our income tax forms on Friday, the thirteenth. That would be double jeopardy!

I hope I don't act dumb. I hope I have gathered up all of my part of the records that we will need. I think that I have written down all of the questions whose answers I need to know. I don't want J. to ask, "How could you possibly forget that? Everybody is supposed to keep up with those!" Or, "You may be right, but that's a complicated way of getting the answer. A much simpler way would be. . . . " Of course I must watch myself too, though, for that approach works both ways. How many times did I used to badger J. saying, "If you would *just* sit down and go through the bank statement when it first arrives. . . . " We even made up a little jingle about that, back in our better days! And I hope J. has forgotten about the time I said, "Dad used to do it this way," only to have a tremendous explosion right back, "I don't care! Your Dad is not always right, even though he thinks he always is!" That was a real losing way to work *together* on our taxes. I want tonight to be serious, civil, to the point, and completely businesslike, without any emotional overloads. If it could be that way, this would be the best income tax time we've ever had. The trouble is that J. and I have not had a very calm way of working together on finances, bookkeeping, and taxes.

Prayer

Dear God, you are my "refuge and strength, a very present help in trouble," and this may be one of those times. I don't want to assume that this evening is going to be trouble, but taxes are never any fun anyway, and money sometimes brings out our worst. I do want to be prepared, not only with my records all in order, but more importantly with myself all in order. I hope that J. is preparing for this evening too. Help us to keep our bad sides under control. And, if we *do* mess up our 1040, or even our emotions a time or two, help us to be calm and to continue working on all these things; for there are matters in life that must be worked through, not around, and this is one of them. May neither one of us exempt ourselves from your presence there. Amen.

19

Freedom

"Who has let the wild ass go free?
Who has loosed the bonds of the swift ass?"
(Job 39:5)

Live as free [persons], yet without using your freedom as a pretext
for evil; but live as servants of God.

(1 Peter 2:16)

An opposite-sex friend has asked me to go to the beach week after next. Several other couples will be going, some of whom are married, some of whom are not. I don't know the ground rules. Is sex assumed or not? How do you ask that in a decent sort of way? We haven't been sex partners up to this point, and I don't know if accepting the invitation would be accepting that part now or not. Maybe it really will be just a low-keyed week, where I won't have to make such a choice immediately; but can I assume that?

I'm an old-fashioned person who is unsure how to play the game in this fast new world come of age. I'm tempted to ask another friend how to handle this, but I always feel silly about having to ask so many child-parent questions. It seems to me that this has been one of my main problems, wanting someone else to tell me what to do.

I'm free, gloriously free! I don't have to ask anyone's permission to do anything. I can go anywhere I want and have a wonderful, satisfying time, and I can also go anywhere I want and have a miserable, self-defeating time. I am free to have fun and to be my own determiner of what is "fun." I am free to fail and to be miserable. I am free to learn on my own, out of my own living experience, without having my ex-spouse, or a counselor, or anyone else in all of creation, telling me what is "best" for me. I wonder if a divorcing person can borrow that cry of Martin Luther King, Jr.: "Free at last! Thank God Almighty, I'm free at last!"

Prayer

Loving God, I am ashamed to admit it to anyone else but you, but the truth is that in this slick, fast world, I am scared to death of this freedom that I had thought was going to be so good. Always before, having a spouse around offered a convenient person to blame for some of the things I did wrong. Now I can only blame myself. Rules and regulations and commandments and conscience—I'm not sure I want to kick all of these over. They are not there just to keep us from destroying other people and valuable property; they also keep us from hurting ourselves. I may be terribly hurt by this beach trip, but then again I may not. In Jesus Christ you were a man for all seasons, and conditions, and circumstances, completely set free. Out of your experience can you give me a sign here, or do I have to look just within myself? If it's the latter, I don't trust myself. Especially not now. Would it be wrong to pray for something like an abscessed tooth, the chickenpox, anything, for an excuse not to go? If you are the Way, please show me. Amen.

20

The Nashville Sound

He who sings songs to a heavy heart
is like one who takes off a garment on a cold day,
and like vinegar on a wound.

(Proverbs 25:20)

A friend of mine once said to me, "You ought to listen to hillbilly music. The music itself is awful, but the lyrics have more honesty in them than almost anything you can ever read." Lately I've been paying attention to his observation. I find myself turning the radio dial to pick up "the Nashville Sound." For me there's a big wave of nostalgia in it too, because I remember how my grandparents always used to tune in to "The Grand Old Opry" with Roy Acuff, Ernest Tubb, Minnie Pearl, and that great voice of a hundred breaking hearts, Hank Williams.

Broadway show tunes are full of optimism, young love, and enthusiasm with a high kick, and that's the kind of image many of us have been nurtured on. However, the Nashville Sound is more like where life is really going on. Most of the lyrics are about lost relationships, broken dreams, unsuccessful attempts to mend, unfaithful spouses, tragic consequences. And the singers neither warble in the manner of a crooner, nor belt it out like a chorus, nor scream in the fashion of today's rock stars. Their hearts mourn, and their voices catch with a sob. Their sad music whines, the words intensely honest. They need no tinsel and glitter, no flashing lights and stunning sets. Just a dark background and a spotlight that sears into the soul.

That music is about me. Probably I could not take too much of it for a steady diet, but right now I find that I really do appreciate it tremendously. I recognize its honesty, for that is where I am. Come to think of it, I wonder if its honesty is part of the reason my unpretentious grandparents seemed to like it when none of the rest of the family could understand why they listened to it all the time. I wonder where those words touched them?

Prayer

God, in Jesus Christ you wept, wept over Lazarus whose relationship with Martha and Mary and you had been broken. You wept over Jerusalem which was so determined to go her own self-destructive way that she could never listen to, or observe, your way, which would have meant life. You listened when the morning stars sang together with your creating ways. You also listen to the sad songs of your hurting people and cry with them. As a hurting person, I thank you for being my kind of God. Hank Williams and Tammy Wynette may describe me, but only you can save me, and for that I am very grateful. "We have heard the joyful sound!" But you have heard the sorrowing cries, and therein lies my real hope. Lest I become too preoccupied with my own sorrows, teach me how to be alert to the sights and sounds of other grieving people as well. That includes J., whom I could not continue living with, but for whom I can still truly pray, even as I pray for myself. Amen.

21

Old Family Photos

Say not, "Why were the former days better than these?"
For it is not from wisdom that you ask this.

(Ecclesiastes 7:10)

I was almost prepared for this one, since all the books and the counselors warn you about coming to grips with the family photograph albums and slide collections. Forewarned is forearmed, or so they say. Who gets which ones? And what do you do about the ones you both want, and the occasional ones you would like to cut down the middle and keep only half?

Our family photos are like the stop-action shots the sports broadcasters now do so well. The media technicians "freeze" the action and even enlarge the scene for better viewing. That's all right for shots from what was once our living relationship (living? I think so). One friend told me that their pictures had been such poignant reminders of *both* the good and the bad that she had given away far too many, or else had thrown away too many others entirely. Careful now. Later on I might want some of those pictures which trouble me now. Or, if I don't want them, someone else in the family might.

Stop-action is something I can eventually take, I think. Maybe I can even now, if I'm careful. What I don't want is any instant replays! I think this analogy has broken down, but you get the idea of what I mean. I can begin to look at something, provided I also don't have to relive it.

Prayer

"God of the past, our times are in Thy hand." That's good to remember; but I must admit that I get a little shaky when I hold these bits and pieces of my (our) past, and it suddenly seems to me that "our times are in my hand." Help me to grow to understand that whatever yesterday was or wasn't, you are the only power that really holds the past. J. doesn't and neither do I; neither do our respective families before us. And, since you are the only one holding yesterday, I can trust that you're always ready to forgive it and to redeem it so that I—indeed both of us—can handle its reminders and their meanings and build upon such again. And once this happens, maybe the photographs can just become nostalgic chronicles of yesterday instead of emotional levers affecting today and tomorrow.

Have I reasoned this one through carefully enough to convince me that it's true? Can I count on it? I'm sure I can count on you. That's the least I know. It may also be the most I know. Amen.

22

My In-law

*. . . and Orpah kissed her mother-in-law, but Ruth clung to her.
. . . Ruth said, "Entreat me not to leave you or to return from
following you; for where you go I will go, and where you lodge I
will lodge; your people shall be my people."*

(Ruth 1:14, 16)

Tomorrow is J.'s mother's birthday. She always seemed to appreciate the birthday cards that I picked out for her, and we often spoke about our not being the typical in-laws in our feelings for one another. What should I do about her birthday this year? My quarrels were with J., not J.'s mother. I like that woman very much; no, it's more than that—I love her.

But our essential link was through J. Does that mean that I am now divorced from her too? I think so. The cleaner those ties are cut, probably the better. What about her husband? What about my parents? All of us used to talk about our being "one, big, happy family," with good connections everywhere. Now our part of that big, happy family is all messed up, even if the others are intact. I realized, of course, that we would never have those big Thanksgiving dinners together anymore—with both sides of the family sitting down together, including several unattached uncles and aunts—but the present ambiguities are much more complex than simply no longer having a family holiday meal.

I'm learning more and more about divorce. There's always talk about how it affects the children, but there's a lot more to it than that. It affects parents and aunts and uncles and lots and lots of each other's friends and neighbors and relatives, seemingly *ad infinitum*. And it sneaks up on you, like the other day when Ellen was talking to me and started to say, "Tell J. that I'm looking forward to (her/his) fixing the family punch at my next birthday party." And then she stopped in a fluster somewhere in the middle of her sentence, whereupon I tried to extricate her. There just for a moment she had forgotten that J. and I aren't married to each other anymore, and among other things it means that asking *me* about J.'s "family punch" is inappropriate now. Should I try to find a family punch from my side of our erstwhile home and offer it to her? Probably not. There are no such things as "instant family traditions," especially ones created to offset others.

Prayer

Our Father—my Father—you put us into the midst of families, and you came to live in the midst of a family too. When you left that family, you made sure that Mary was taken care of by John. I'm leaving some dear family members and friends. Who is going to care for them?

You've been along this way before. Can you help me know how to handle my separation feelings, since I care a great deal for these people? Is there no end of my grief? I would like to pray for my in-laws in this matter as well, for my hunch is that they are having problems with this, just as I am. I want us to be able to deal with each other out front in these cloudy issues, and in order to do so, we all need to be honest. I surely do need some guidance as to how to make this happen. Amen.

23

A Wedding Anniversary

Come, let us take our fill of love till morning;
let us delight ourselves with love.

(Proverbs 7:18)

Next Sunday is Uncle Ned's and Aunt Bertha's fiftieth wedding anniversary and there's going to be a big reception in the fellowship hall at the church. I guess I ought to buy them a present and a card; and I suppose I should at least put in an appearance at the celebration, though I don't want to be an embarrassment to such good folks.

The truth is that I hate marital success stories (at least I do right now). I haven't always been that way. Of course I'm envious! They're having what I can never have. Does that mean that God is blessing them more than me? If so, I'm sure they deserve it more than I. Or, does this milestone mean that they are truly better people? No, that can't be true, because Dr. and Mrs. McLeod were the "best" people I've ever known, and they were both killed in an automobile accident just a month short of their twenty-fifth wedding anniversary. They were truly good people with a wonderful marriage (I think).

God doesn't give out marriage blessings, i.e., success pronouncements, on the basis of seniority, or on a basis of righteousness.

Still, Uncle Ned and Aunt Bertha do have a wonderful record. Do you suppose they ever thought about divorce in all those years? They're bound to have done so, only folks never, ever verbalized those feelings openly in their generation, unless someone's conduct was so blatantly scandalous as to be impossible to sweep under the rug. Then they used such silly terms as "the innocent party" and the "guilty party."

We all ought to be proud of Uncle Ned and Aunt Bertha. A good marriage. A long marriage. 50 years. 600 months. 2,600 weeks. That's more than 18,250 days—and nights. Over 438,000 hours.

Wait a minute, this is getting ridiculous. I'm doing the very thing I said God doesn't do! I guess at a time like this I'm embarrassed by the low numbers of the statistics in my own case. What you really count (or can't count) are how many times Bertha laughed at Ned's tired old jokes, and how many times Ned pleasantly ate those biscuits that never were very good, and how many times they cried, laughed, failed, fought, and made love together.

I can't begrudge them all those things. They have something to celebrate. I'll certainly go there gladly. Besides, folks will probably and properly be focusing on them, not me. There aren't as many people concerned over my divorce as I sometimes like to think there are.

Prayer

Lord, I'm grateful for Uncle Ned and Aunt Bertha's long, useful married life. Some of the old-timers have known a lot more about living and loving than the rest of us have. And I'm glad your Word suggests that on the fiftieth year we all celebrate a Jubilee! It will be good to be jubilant with them! Amen.

24

A Good Memory

I consider the days of old,
I remember the years long ago.
(Psalm 77:5)

Even the darkness is not dark to thee.
(Psalm 139:12)

I had been wanting to go back up to Panther Mountain at sundown for a long time, because that has to be one of the most breathtaking scenes I've ever experienced. The trouble was that the mountain was *also* the place where we agreed that we wanted to get married and "live happily ever after." Still later, in a truly romantic, nostalgic gesture, we went back up there for the ritualistic putting on of the diamond—although of course it had been tried on many times at the store.

Dare I go back to a place which has so many memories of events that were related to the making of a marriage which subsequently came unmade? Can I handle this power of the past?

"Certainly!", I reasoned. "I had been going up there for years before our engagement. In fact I had gone there with some other dates, before J. came along and claimed it as 'our special place.' Why should I let that unique association with the mountain get in the way? Sometimes I'm too sentimental for my own good!"

I went last evening, even though I could not quite rationalize all the reasons I wanted to go. It was just as lovely as I remembered. I'd be lying if I said that I managed to push J. completely out of my mind, but at the same time I tuned in to lots of other memories associated with that place. For instance, one summer evening when I was seventeen years old, Dad took me up there with him to talk and renew companionship, when things weren't quite right between us. I drove up there to be by myself when Grandma died. The summer after I finished college I even tried to paint the scene from the mountain on canvas—disaster!

Yes, last night, as the stars were coming out in the evening sky over Panther Mountain, I got back in touch with some mighty nice things about myself. It was part worship, part catharsis, part nostalgia, part proving something to myself—and all good.

The sun was totally gone; the oranges and pinks and purples were gently sliding together into dusk gray. Feeling good all over, I turned to leave and saw a couple kissing each other. As I walked back down to my car, I didn't blame them a bit; I've always found Panther Mountain to be a love place, even though sometimes it does put a little mist in your eyes.

Prayer

God of memories, I'm such a creature of memories. That's one of the bonds existing between you and me. Memories also bind me to lots of other people. Since you and I are engaged in memory together, I'm counting on your help in smoothing over some of my ragged ones. I made a beginning with one of them this evening. Thank you—very much. Amen.

25

The Security of Someone Else

Do not be afraid of sudden panic, . . .
for the LORD will be your confidence
and will keep your foot from being caught.
(Proverbs 3:25, 26)

Today I backed into a sharp corner of the wall can opener in the kitchen. I scratched myself on the dumb thing, and I needed a band-aid—only I could not reach the place that was bleeding. I had to let it coagulate on its own, and I finally managed to get a tissue in place on it. Still later a friend at work put a bandage on it for me.

I know it's a little thing, but it made me think about lots of other far more critical times that I might need someone to help me, only now there won't be anybody nearby. I guess that's one of the comforts of marriage, even a less-than-perfect marriage. There's someone around to help when you are sick, or when you're dizzy, or when you sprain an ankle; and what person living alone hasn't thought about waking up with the realities of a heart attack and wondering if it will be possible to phone for the rescue squad? Dad wouldn't be alive today if Mother hadn't been right there in the bedroom with him when he had that massive heart attack two years ago. If the same thing were to happen to me tonight, would I survive? Or if I were to die in my sleep tonight, would I be found?

Still, the fear of not having help when you are sick or dying is certainly no reason for a person to stay married. We were having far more opportunities to wound each other with our words and attitudes and deeds than we would ever have chances to save one another's life. Besides, what would be the purpose of saving someone just to have more of the same kind of life we already had? That would be sadistic! Yet the truth is that, when you're sick or frightened or injured or grieving, there is a certain security in having someone there. I might not have been completely tender and caring toward J. there at the end, but at least I would not have allowed my companion to die, unattended and abandoned to fate.

Prayer

Dear Lord, what's happening to me? I'm feeling sorry for myself—I want somebody always handy to help me out. You're called "a very present help in trouble." You're even called a Savior. What do those words mean for a divorced person? Can you save me from being afraid? Can you save me from myself? Amen.

26

Analysis

. . . and let me not be put to shame in my hope.
(Psalm 119:116)

Today I made an appointment with a psychiatrist. Everybody (Who's *everybody*? Sometimes I sound like a parent of a teenager refuting peer pressures) says that divorcing people ought to get themselves a counselor, or else get into a support group or a therapy group. These resources are supposed to help me analyze what went wrong, to get an objective picture of how I really come across, and to begin to suggest how I might start moving away from being the kind of person who made relational living unsatisfactory while moving toward becoming a more fulfilling individual, whether I marry again or not. That's a big order to lay on a doctor who at this point is only a name recommended to me by a friend who found him helpful in similar circumstances.

I'm scared about this appointment. I never did like to undress in front of a doctor, and this undressing is likely to be much more embarrassing and shivery than any I've ever known before now.

I've read some material about this, so I'm at least familiar with some of the language. For instance, there is the maxim: "True self-discovery comes only when we begin to disclose ourselves to someone else." And there are phrases: "Removing one's masks"; "doing something about one's self-defeating behavioral patterns"; "getting rid of the filters which interfere with our perception of reality." It would be nice if I could do all that. Or if the doctor could. Or if God could.

Reappraisal and self-analysis are psychological terms, but can they be faith terms too? Are those terms kin to contrition, repentance, confession, redemption, "being saved?" That's it: I want to be saved. Not from J., but from me. From a bad past, an uncertain present, a threatening future. I want to be an integrated whole person, like God intended me to be: open, trusting, caring, giving, receiving, growing, being filled up and overflowing. Getting there looms as such an awesome, fearful struggle.

Prayer

Lord, what must I do to be saved? Get into therapy? Somehow or other, that doesn't quite sound like what the familiar Bible verse truly meant. Can the gospel of Jesus Christ, which redeems a person and makes that individual whole again, work through the counseling process? I'm counting on it, Lord. But I realize that claiming my faith resources is important too. I am not going to undress myself in anybody's presence without the certainty of your presence being there as well. You always have an appointment with me, and you can count on my counting on you. Amen.

27

The Checkbook

"Behold, no fear of me need terrify you;
my pressure will not be heavy upon you."
(Job 33:7)

It is such a simple-looking thing: a vinyl snap folder enclosing twenty-five little sheets of paper measuring only about three by six inches. It does not look like a battlefield, but it certainly has been. That was mainly because of the existence of the word *or* between our names on the account—an *or* whose very existence implied that a lot of conversation was going on between us, but which was not; an *or* whose presence assumed that some conflicting values had been discussed and either compromised or worked out to the surrendering person's satisfaction; an *or* which assumed that someone was in charge and that a two-headed financial unit was indeed a unit, not a monster or a schizophrenic disease.

All of these assumptions were ill-founded. Management of our financial affairs was one of those things we did not discuss in the beginning of our marriage, and consequently we never did get around to talking about it, at least not reasonably. By the time we admitted that our "Mr. or Mrs." account needed some kind of professional financial counsel, we were locked into our respective positions, each very certain that the only effectual counsel would be for the benefit of the other person.

It all seems like such a simple matter when I reflect on it now. There was no earthly reason for us to argue so much about our finances. (No, that's not right; there were *two* quite earthly reasons, and two stubborn ones at that: J. and I.) I do not remember our ever discussing and agreeing on how best to handle our money. Each of us just picked up the checkbook, under the authority of that *or,* and then we proceeded to act by that authority pretty much as each one of us pleased; and such unilateral moves rarely pleased the other.

Not only did we work out of two different bases, with few common agreements; but also, I will have to admit, I often complicated the matter by neglecting to fill in the check stubs. I can't blame the blank stubs on J. Almost every one of them was my doing, or rather my not doing. Of course, I insisted that on an unconscious level I was purposely trying to be frustrating to a meticulously exacting spouse. And, even when I kept them filled, my subtraction was sometimes shoddy.

Prayer

Wise and glorious God, why is it that *good* people turn into such stupid people under certain predictable circumstances? I am very sorry that I made things difficult in this area of life. Whether I did it intentionally or carelessly, the effect was the same. Sometimes I wonder why you hang in there with us, and ultimately why you hung up there for us. Even though I don't understand your reasons, I thank you for doing so. It's a comfort in my confused, mixed-up world. Amen.

28

Reduced Finances

"I become afraid of all my suffering."
(Job 9:28)

*Those who were brought up in purple
lie on ash heaps.*
(Lamentations 4:5)

We lived a lot better when we were married to one another than either of us can now live apart. Two can't live more cheaply than one, but two can definitely live together with less expenses than those same two people can live apart. I guess that's the whole rationale behind so many group houses and communal homes today.

That's one of the things that makes me angry about our divorce! There ought to be numerous disappointments and angers that are higher on the list than the economic one, but it seems that it is the one that rises up to smite me the most often! We may not have had a very good marriage, but we did have a good "logistical support system," as one of my friends used to call her defunct marriage.

I've got less money to spend at the same time it is costing me more money simply to live. That means I have less money to use for my own pleasure. Is that a part of God's "punishment" for my "sin?" My Calvinist forebears would certainly have thought so. If they are right, then God is going to catch it too, because I've obviously got less money to give to the church and to charity! I realize that we are supposed to give the firstfruits, but if I gave off the top of my now reduced resources, I might not have enough left to survive. Or, at least, that's the way it feels to me right now.

The truth, of course, is that I got used to a lot of things that went along with our married lifestyle, and while the two of us took deliberate steps to get unmarried, neither one of us has taken very many steps to get "unlifestyled." And, because both of us are selfish enough not to want to make those adjustments, J. and I both direct anger toward each other as being responsible for the financial squeeze we find ourselves in.

The truth is that each of us can live more simply and still survive. We just don't *want* to do that. And it's easier to get mad at the other person as the causer of all this than to shape up within oneself.

Prayer

Great God, from whom comes all good things, chief of all, the gift of our salvation in Christ, I have been abundantly gifted, far above deserving—though admittedly not above desiring. I know that. What I need is the patient courage to live my changed life with prudence and care. In the process maybe I can learn a lesson that a number of people living elsewhere in this world already know—that wealth is not necessarily measured in economic terms. Help me to take a hard look at where my real treasures are, for that is where I want my heart to be also. I pray in the name of him who became poor that I might become rich. Amen.

29

My Sexual Self

. . . my loins are filled with burning.
(Psalm 38:7)

This morning I masturbated. I hadn't really planned to, and it wasn't any big to-do. I simply did it. It was a lazy Saturday morning, and I was still in bed, about half asleep. I began thinking that this was a time when we nearly always used to make love. I recalled especially that Saturday of the big snow, winter before last. Then, the next thing I knew, I wasn't simply remembering; I was reliving (relief-ing?).

Those were powerful feelings, both during and afterwards. Of course, it wasn't the first time I had done that since we separated, and it won't be the last. (The truth is I did it while we were still living together, too.)

Doing that can be one way of coping with loneliness. It helps for a little while. I'm not going to feel guilty about it. Better to do that than to pretend that I don't have any sexual feelings, simply because I no longer have a partner. Rigid continence would require a degree of self-control, which I don't have, and it might drive in to me a kind of tension that wouldn't make for very healthy living either. Also, better these private moments than a meaningless series of promiscuous moments. Doing it won't give you VD; nor does it make someone else's marriage partner unfaithful; and we've long since gotten away from thinking it made you crazy.

Sexual relief, however, is only a partial answer to a human predicament. An orgasm is no substitute for a sexual relationship, where there is giving and receiving, and moments when you don't know which is which. And most of all, when there's a person there with you, life is momentarily filled up. Even though I recognize all this, I still have to admit that this morning was okay. I am learning to "go with" some of the good things in my feelings and my fantasies. At the same time, I must remember that this must not obscure the fact that the ultimate goal of a Christian sexual expression is to give someone else a wholeness—not simply to receive one's personal pleasure.

Prayer

Dear God, thank you for complex glands and body fluids and nerve endings, all of which you made and pronounced "good"; and thank you for private moments, and precious memories, and flights of fantasy. Help me to remember that when I use these for myself alone, that's just a stopgap measure for dealing with that world of reality where you are always trying to help me be at home. I'm glad that you are a God who isn't afraid to live in every area of my world and in every part of myself. Amen.

30

A Dream

I slept, but my heart was awake.
(Song of Solomon 5:2)

It happened again. I dreamed about J. I do that a lot. Most of the time the two of us are enjoying ourselves in those dreams. Once, however, I dreamed we were trying to kill each other. Several times I've dreamed that we were both falling in slow motion through space, but with the ability to maneuver ourselves around in spite of the pull of gravity. This latest dream was more practical. We were dividing up some kitchen items, and rather than giving me the blender I wanted, J. threw it out the door and said that I didn't know how to blend very well anyway, or we wouldn't be separating. That's when I woke up.

Before we were married I used to dream a lot about J. Fun dreams. Crazy dreams. Erotic dreams. But now my night life, like my day life, seems to be a series of nightmares. Why can't I simply sleep and be done with it? Goodness knows, I need the rest. Why must I keep dealing with this person and this situation even when I am trying to sleep? Is God punishing me? A counselor would probably say that J. and I needed to talk to one another about our respective dreams, looking at all the unresolved issues they are communicating to us. Hah! If we had talked to one another about all our dreams a long time ago—and if we had listened—we might not be where we are today!

The Bible says that in the kingdom days, "Your sons and your daughters shall prophesy,/your old men shall dream dreams,/and your young men shall see visions" (Joel 2:28). It does not say that in the kingdom days "your divorcing children shall have nightmares." Does that mean that God is absent from my nightmares, or maybe that divorcing people are not really kingdom folks? I don't think so, but what *does* it mean? It does not seem fair to me that J. should be sneaking up on me while I have put it all out of my mind. Obviously I have not really done that. What now?

Prayer

Gracious God, my whole life seems like one big nightmare. Why do my nights have to be more of the same? I remember your reassurance after Jacob's dream: "Behold, I am with you and will keep you wherever you go. . . . " And look at how he had loused up his family relationships! If you can reassure me in that same kind of way, then I won't worry so much about my dreams or their supposed meanings. And I give you the safekeeping of my future dreams. Those are the ones I can still do something about. Amen.

31

Weight Loss

My body has become gaunt.
(Psalm 109:24)

I forget to eat my bread.
(Psalm 102:4)

My tears have been my food day and night.
(Psalm 42:3)

I've lost three more pounds without meaning to! Divorcing seems to be a more efficient way to slim down than either dieting or exercise. But it's an awful way to lose, since you are losing a great deal more than inches and pounds; you are losing a lot of yourself.

Various people have noticed my weight loss and have commented about it. My clothes hang loosely on me; my color is bad; I feel tired all the time. Part of the reason is because I simply don't seem to have any appetite. I have to make myself eat. Life in general isn't very tasty to me right now. I don't eat balanced meals; I just grab a bite hither and yon, usually on the run.

I heard one of the women at work saying that after her divorce she wore a bra two sizes smaller than before! One friend told me that he developed colitis during his divorce; another, an ulcer; another *gained* twenty pounds from eating too many sweets (and probably from drinking too much). Everyone knows a woman's menstrual cycle is apt to go haywire under such stress; I've even heard of several folks whose hair came out in clumps! It seems ironic that, in order to get healthy, you have to get unhealthy in the process. Maybe this is like Dickens' ". . . the best of times . . . the worst of times."

Thank goodness, I have noticed that J. doesn't look too good either! I would hate to be the only one of us showing signs of suffering. One of the things we both took for granted in our marriage was that at some levels we looked after one another rather well. We ate decent meals. One of us would pick up the other's prescription. If something wasn't quite right about each other's appearance, it was noticed in the "safety" of home before an outsider saw it—like that time I had a seam out of my shorts, only I hadn't noticed it in my haste of dressing for the office picnic.

Now my only "checkpoint friend" at home is my mirror, where, as a typical beholder, I see what I want to see. But even I cannot miss the circles under my eyes, the loose skin hanging on my neck. I must take more responsibility for my health care. That means deliberate slowdowns in some areas of my life, like taking time for a good breakfast, not just a cup of coffee, and a sit-down balanced meal in the evening, rather than depending on carryout junk food.

Prayer

Creator God, you made my body after your own image. That means I'm godly. Help me not to treat that wonderful nature so casually, allowing life to press me and to toss me at will. Show me how to take time to take care of myself in this difficult season. When I make good-health resolutions, give me the will power to follow through. Don't let me become my own worst enemy. I've already had enough experience at doing that! And help J. realize these things too. Amen.

32

Ennui

My strength fails because of my misery,
and my bones waste away.
(Psalm 31:10)

Anxiety in a [person's] heart weighs [her/him] down.
(Proverbs 12:25)

It seems to me that last weekend didn't even happen. I can hardly remember doing anything productive. It was a lost weekend, only not like the Ray Milland movie classic. I didn't lose this one to the bottle; I mainly lost it to myself—feeling sorry for myself with no one to bolster me, not even with assurances of half-truths. Or for that matter, there was no one to push me into doing something, either by strong suggestion or by staying so busy that I would be shamed into activity for my very survival! I also lost the weekend through dissolution into different directions. I can't remember ever having this kind of weekend before we separated. I just couldn't get my act together.

I didn't purposely set out to be lazy. In fact I got up bright and early on Saturday; sleeping in for half the day was not my problem. But it seemed as if everything else was!

First I couldn't find the shoes I wanted to wear. Then there wasn't enough milk for cereal. I couldn't find the grocery list I had already made out, so when I went shopping it was by memory—and of course I omitted a half-dozen things, which I recalled at various times later during the day. When I returned to the store, I still didn't wind up with everything. I sat down to pay bills, and my checkbook had only two checks. The ones I had ordered had not arrived, so now I will have to go by the bank to have some temporary ones issued. The car needed inspection, but I had to buy a new tire first. By the time I was ready to get in line at the inspection station, I realized that it would take much too long. I ate Saturday supper by myself at Wendy's. I watched an old movie on TV and planned to vacuum the place afterwards but by then I felt too tired. I went on to bed early. I read a paperback for a while but it was boring. On Sunday morning I went to church, but I decided not to go to my regular one. On a whim I went out to Trinity Church instead. The tenors were flat, and the minister was worse. And no one spoke to me except the usher when I arrived and the pastor when I left. And the latter, in repeating my name, mispronounced it.

This was a wasted weekend. I felt almost paralyzed, and time itself seemed equally heavy and unmoving.

Prayer

If you are so providential, God, why did you send me such a loser of a weekend? I needed something zippier. Some of those things were my fault; others just happened. The depressing point is, I didn't seem to have psychic or physical energy to cope with any of them. I think I really would have been better off staying in bed all weekend. Help me to think through these times better beforehand, and to have some optional plans to fall back on when I recognize one of these times upon me. Amen.

33

A Remarriage to One Another

Speak tenderly to Jerusalem,
and cry to her
that her warfare is ended.
(Isaiah 40:2)

That really shook me up! Jack and Susan were remarried last week, to each other, mind you, nearly six years after they had been divorced. "We agreed that the divorce was the worst mistake we had ever made, and we finally saw no good reason to keep living with that mistake." There was a big bash over at the Boyds' house, complete with a minister and hired musicians. They had invited all of their old friends, including J. and me. We talked it over on the phone. I didn't think either one of us ought to go, even though one of us might attend separately. No use our unwittingly giving out the possibility of our reconciliation too. Typically, J. felt that I was being overly sensitive and a bit paranoid, but I didn't budge on this one. J. probably went, but I certainly did not. It's been too difficult arriving at our decisions so far; I saw no reason either to embarrass Jack and Susan with our lack of re-connection, or to be uncomfortable because they were back together. And I certainly did not want the first person to come up to me and say, "I sure do hope that maybe you and J. might also . . ."

I don't understand you, Jack and Susan! Why are you doing this to me? Divorced people should stay divorced. I simply don't have the capacity to live with as many ambiguities as some people seem capable of managing. My world works best when I can keep people and relationships in their proper "boxes." Jack and Susan have just turned a part of that world upside down, and I don't like it. Suppose it's catching, like the measles? What does it mean to live in a world where people and things won't stay put where we can get used to them? Why do you suppose J. wasn't especially bothered at the prospect of going to that particular re-wedding?

Prayer

Dear God, please don't let me be this way. Those folks are who they are, and we are who we are. Who's to say there's any carryover there? I like Jack and Susan, and I pray for them. I rejoice that their reconciliation, healing, and remarriage has occurred, and that they were able to recognize it, so that now they can be truly one—maybe even more so than they were to begin with. Bless them, and may they go on from strength to strength! Meanwhile, back here in our unmended state, I pray also for J. and me, not that this same thing might happen, but that each of us may also be truly healed, however you will it. Keep me open to the signs of this sure thing that I know you will provide. Amen.

34

A Familiar Item

Then he remembered the days of old . . .
(Isaiah 63:11)

It was bound to happen sooner or later. I guess there will probably be more of this sort of thing, but it certainly came as a surprise this first time around. I needed a favorite little pan for something I was cooking. I looked all around for it, thinking that I must be getting really careless and forgetful, and then I remembered that this was one of the things that J. had kept.

We readily agreed how most of our household items should be divided, since many of them were especially identified with one or the other of us. But the common properties—they were something else. In my haste to get it all over with, I probably gave over to J. too many of them. Like that pan—I really was attached to that little pan. My mother had one almost exactly like it that I had used that first time I tried to fix my parents their breakfast in bed. Why should such a pan now be with J., who never used it that much anyway? I wonder if I ought to ask for it back, or would I look silly doing that this late in the game?

There are a lot of items we once shared together that I assumed we would always have. I had taken them for granted. That pan seems very important to me now, all out of proportion to reality, as if it were a central part of my life. I wonder how many other things there are like that? As I remember their absence, how will I cope?

Prayer

Dear God, you know what it's like to give away a part of yourself to someone else. The Scripture speaks of your emptying yourself. There's a lot of me that has been emptied out for somebody else's life and well being. I don't think I like all of these tugging reminders, and part of me wants most of these things back again. At the very least, I need help understanding how this longing for the familiar can be a good thing. How can I move beyond this present state? Will you please show me? Amen.

35

Self-image

I have become like a broken vessel.
(Psalm 31:12)

I have failed in one of the most important experiences of life. True, I didn't fail all by myself, but I *have* failed. It may take me months, and even years, to recover.

Nobody in our family has ever failed. My great grandfather, the banker, even weathered the Depression intact. And two other sets of great-grandparents kept their farm during those bleak days. Even Dad's Uncle Hoyt put together a shoe repair shop that made it back then, in spite of all sorts of dire predictions. My grandmother was Phi Beta Kappa and May Queen both! My brother was editor of his law review in graduate school. I was president of the student body my senior year in college.

Nobody fails in our family; and, predictably, I married someone who comes from a long line of non-failures too. And yet, together we failed, and separately we failed too. We may be the first ones in either family ever to do that. At least, that's the way it feels to me right now.

My self-esteem is deflated. I continue to go through all the motions of living, but right now life is just a mechanical treadmill. I liked who I thought I was, but now I don't know who I am anymore, or where I'm going. I understand, now, why few problems are greater than lowered self-esteem.

I am having to surrender my idealized image of my successful self-sufficiency, and I am having to learn about my real self. I suspect that J. is going through much of the same too, although of course we don't talk about it. The pain in learning about myself comes in realizing how far apart my two images—the projected one and the real one—have been all through the years. I've always been on the edge of failure, and only by working hard have I managed to avoid it. Not this time, however. In fact, on this one I may have failed simply because I did *not* work hard. I know how to work hard on projects, but the same dynamic doesn't necessarily work on people—on myself.

I worry if my family and friends will like the "new me" as well as I thought they liked the "old me". Will *I* like this me? Can I learn to live with a more realistic me? Or will I divorce myself from *that* me too? I hope not.

Prayer

Cross-bound Savior, help me to know that it's all right to fail. Some even say that you did: "He saved others; he cannot save himself." What does that mean for me? You have said, "Blessed are the pure in heart," not "blessed are the pure in history." Both J. and I need to be reminded of this gospel truth. So do our families. May it be so! You have promised that each of us can be a new creation in you, losing our every dis-ease. Make my new creation safe in your gentle arms. Amen.

36

The Bathroom

Your eyes will see strange things,
and your mind utter perverse things.
(Proverbs 23:33)

Glory be! My bathroom is all mine! I wonder how many divorces start in the bathroom instead of in the bedroom? Our marriage had some great moments in the bedroom, but even from the very beginning we never did have a good marriage in the bathroom.

One of us was forever staying in there too long. Neither was diligent about cleaning out the tub after using it. Dripping pantyhose and mangled toothpaste tubes were not our particular problems. But we disagreed about the propriety of one of us going in to use the toilet while the other one was in the shower or at the basin. And, as ridiculous as it sounds, we had been raised in respective homes where toilet paper was hung differently; "over" and "under" became magnified as symbols of family honor and which one of us had received the "right" parenting! Also, the medicine cabinet was far too cluttered with out-of-date prescriptions and bottled paraphernalia of dubious usefulness. And, oh yes, I invariably forgot to turn on the exhaust fan, which irked J. no end.

Now, my bathroom is all mine, to do *with* as I want, and to do *in* as I want. Only, there are so many moments when that sovereignty feels like such hollow victory. Such as this morning when I threw up twice, and there was no one on the other side of the door, checking to see if I was okay, no one getting me a glass of water, no one cleaning up the splatter afterwards when I still felt a bit woozy. Now when I run out of razor blades, there's none to swipe from the other person! I even remember—and miss—the spontaneous response I used to get from J. when I impishly soaped a sexy come-on on the mirror, which could be read when the condensate had formed around the letters while J.

was taking a shower! It was one of our few safe bathroom jokes, the one that could not raise the other's ire. Sharing a bathroom *can* be fun. It's one of the most personable places I know of. I've got plenty of time and space in mine now, but there are times when I miss having that other person in it with me, or before me, or after me.

Besides, when I'm in there now, who's going to answer the phone?

Prayer

Dear God, you made us in such fashion that we need to do all sorts of very personal activities in the bathroom. When we were living together the bathroom was one place where we didn't try very hard to work out our shared functions and relationships. Some of our disagreements there seem silly now. The truth is that I would do many things differently, if I just had an opportunity. I appreciate my bodily humanity, which you made, but I never allowed myself to appreciate J.'s humanity in that same place, one that my spouse handled with more privacy than I. I miss the possibility of both individual privacy and shared privacy. If I ever share such a space again, teach me to distinguish between privacy and loneliness. Amen.

37

Talking and Listening

A fool multiplies words.
(Ecclesiastes 10:14)

It seems to me that I have been talking to myself far more during these last couple of weeks than I have usually done. That is something I had not figured on. I wonder if this is normal for someone in my circumstances?

Of course it's not as if I had not been doing a lot of that already. With J. around, you might just as well as have been talking to yourself most of the time, for all of the real communicating that was going on! Yet we also lived around one another with long periods of silence as well, and were often afraid to speak because of the reaction that might produce. Now I find that often I want to talk to someone, but now I don't even have the option of someone around, listening or not. On the other hand, when I am around people, I'm just as likely to withdraw and choose not to talk, even when I have the chance. And many times I really don't want people to talk to me, especially about our divorce. This talking and listening business has always been a problem with me, and it would seem that now it's more troublesome than ever!

I certainly realize that something I need to work on in my new life is talking in a way that I am being true to what is really inside of me, and speaking in such a way that others truly hear and understand this. And likewise I need to listen carefully to what others are saying, or what they are trying to say. That's something the two of us never really learned to do, in spite of all the time we lived together.

Meanwhile, I am talking in my sleep, talking to myself when I am awake, addressing my mirror image, and constantly thinking out loud. What's the old joke about not worrying about talking to yourself, but that you should begin worrying when you start answering yourself back? Right now I don't see anything especially humorous about that joke. It's something I do all the time.

Prayer

O God, I know that you are concerned with words. You are partly revealed in your written word of Scripture, in your preached word of sermons, in your symbol-word of sacraments, and in Jesus, your complete revelation in a fleshly Word. Much of that will always remain a mystery to each of us, but somewhere in that mystery there is the assurance that words are important ways that you have of letting your feelings and your truth get through. I haven't used my words very well that way in the past. Maybe you can help me learn how to talk to you and to listen to you better than I have done, and from that experience begin to learn how to talk and to listen better to people who are important in my life. I hope so. Amen.

38

Lack of Trust

". . . all my members are like a shadow."
(Job 17:7)

. . . vain is the help of man!
(Psalm 108:12)

I'm discovering that I don't trust anybody anymore, and I realize now that this is interfering with everything I do and with every relationship I have. It all began when I realized I could no longer trust J., who seemed to be doing me in emotionally at every available chance. It probably worked both ways, but naturally it felt like a one-way problem to me.

Because I only believed half the words J. said, my suspicions and cynicism have accelerated in every direction. Now I have trouble believing what my doctor says, what my counselor suggests, what my lawyer advises, what my friends tell me, even what my supervisor tells me about my work.

I'm skeptical about everyone. I assume anyone who tries to get close to me has a hidden agenda. I never accept anything at face value anymore. Feeling that way boxes me in tightly, into a depressed, isolated self. I know it's not healthy. My complexion is breaking out; my intestines growl; more than once I've had diarrhea for no apparent reason.

I'm scared of being vulnerable again, of putting myself out where I can be hurt again or disappointed some more.

I wonder, can trust once broken ever be restored? Yet I believe that's what the Bible story is all about. God trusted Adam and Eve, making them vulnerable to sin, and making holy divinity vulnerable to them. Whatever they did affected God, for Adam and Eve were God's extended-image soul-mates. Theirs was supposed to be the closest, most trusting relationship in the universe. As J. and I were intended. And when the Creator-creation relationship failed, God still trusted humanity in new covenant-making. But I'm not God, who does the impossible and asks us to do it as well.

But when you have given yourself into the trusting relationship of marriage and have been terribly hurt, it's hard to get up and willingly ask for the possibility of being hurt again. How far does God expect me to go? "Until seventy times seven"? (Matthew 18:22, KJV). Does God expect me to make a fool out of myself, simply because it's God's nature to do that?

Prayer

Lord, I'll admit I'm too angry and too disappointed to do much trusting. Trusting is like walking out on a tightrope when there's no safety net and looking up to discover the person holding the other end of the rope is someone whom you are sure is getting ready to jiggle it. In these moments, O Lord, walk with me, and reassure me with the knowledge that underneath are the everlasting arms.

I don't enjoy being cynical. I want to trust again. It may be the only way I can ever really be a whole person and live again. Remind me that not everyone is going to loosen the rope. And since I need trusting human relationships, please show me who the truly trustworthy human beings are, because I need some to depend on. Amen.

39

Self-indulgence

*For you were called to freedom, . . . do not use your freedom as
an opportunity for the flesh.*

(Galatians 5:13)

. . . let me not be put to shame.
(Psalm 25:20)

Divorcing seems to be making lots of alterations in my value
system, even though I keep saying that it does not. I hope some of
these alterations are just temporary preoccupations.

I realize I am becoming much too self-centered. I worry about
myself all the time; I'm not tuned in to other people as well as I once
thought I was. I tend to forget that life goes on and invariably brings a
lot of worries about a lot of other subjects to lots of other people.

I gave up my volunteer work at the local jail. I explained that it
would just be a temporary "recess" while I devoted my energies to
getting my own life back together and out of its own various
imprisonments. Still, once I've gotten out of the rhythm of that
work—which spun off many responsibilities—I wonder if I'll really
ever go back to it? Margaret called last weekend to tell me that they
missed me and hoped I would soon be back. I made a continuing
excuse.

I catch myself looking in the mirror more often, hoping that I look
good, that I will make a good impression. That never used to be such a
preoccupation with me. I was one of the world's original insisters that
the real person is on the inside. Yet, just last week I had my hair cut
differently—just a little change, but a change nonetheless. Yesterday I
picked up some travel brochures for the Bahamas. I also bought a new
plaid blazer, and I've been window-shopping at jewelry stores looking
for a new watch, not exactly sure what I want, but vaguely thinking

that I owe myself something for being such a stalwart, dutiful, decent person in these recent weeks.

I don't understand what's happening to me. Certainly there were many things wrong about the old marriage, but does that mean that whatever remains can be remedied by being spruced up on the outside? It does not seem right that changing partners, or being without one, should necessarily mean changing lifestyles.

Prayer

Who am I, Lord? Who do you want me to be? Am I trying to show J. that my divorced identity is going to be totally different from my married identity? Am I trying to prove to the world that the old me who failed in our marriage is only a relic? that I'm a bright, attractive butterfly emerging from my dead cocoon?

Is this kind of image-polishing self-indulgence the best way to grow at this time? Can a leopard change its spots? God, you never change, "to endless years" you are "the same." Can you help me sort out the important areas where I should stay the same too? I hope so. I don't want to make a fool out of myself. Amen.

40

The Impersonal Form

. . . I would rather not use paper and ink.
(2 John 12)

I must have filled out thousands of such forms during my life, but this time it was different. Today, for the first time, I had to check "Divorced." Always before my answer had been "Single" or "Married." Even during our separation, while the legalities were still in process, I usually finessed that point, rationalizing that *Married*, being technically still a correct answer, was assuredly a safer answer. But yesterday our divorce was final; the papers have all been signed; the judgments rendered. J. and I are divorced, and I must begin to acknowledge that reality, both on paper and in speech.

And inside myself. It seemed strange not to fill in a spouse's name. There was a question about who should be notified in case of an emergency, and there was no one who came immediately to mind. I almost put down J.'s name anyway. Maybe I should have.

I know that filling out that one form on this one particular day did not suddenly make me into a different person, but doing it and seeing it surely made me *feel* like a different person. I didn't like it, but that's a part of what I've got to begin living with from now on. The truth is that I did not like all of my feelings even before we entered our legal proceedings. It's been a long time since I've really been comfortable and have felt at rest with *us,* or with J., or with me. Maybe now that all of this is out there in black and white, I can begin to deal with my life in a more out front manner and, I hope, moving out of all my discomforts and dislikes. It will be good not to feel so fractured. There is a sense in which being divorced may help each of us become more together within our respective selves.

Prayer

O Lord, I remember some lines from an old hymn: "Change and decay in all around I see; O Thou who changest not, abide with me." Those words seem to fit me. So much has changed and still is changing. Nothing seems fixed and settled, least of all me. It's good to remember that you are eternal. I need you, and I need what you represent, especially now, so very much. Amen.

Postscript

These devotions are designed to be reflections. I hope that you are seeing and feeling yourself within them and, more important, that you are seeing and feeling God's presence in them.

Moreover, I am increasingly convinced that it is important for you to see and feel J.'s presence here too. Although it may not always be apparent to you, J.'s fear, ambiguity, pain, and adjustments proceed along just as do your own. Somewhere, somehow, sometime, you can acknowledge this as the person of faith that you are. Perhaps this will come in moments of reflective prayer.

Divorce may be a very personal matter, but it is not a private matter. J. is always there. And I do not believe that true reconciliation will ever come about within you until you and J. and God are all viewed as being there together.

I am not suggesting that you can "help" J., who, after all, must move through the Wilderness at a pace which is appropriate for a different self, different perceptions, and different circumstances. As the old spiritual said so well, "O! Nobody else can walk it for you. You have to walk it for yourself." But God goes with J., even if J. does not always recognize or admit this. God goes with J. just as God goes with you.

I hope that you will increasingly find that you are including J.'s well-being with God in your prayers. When this becomes a "natural" thing for a divorcing Christian to do, then these devotions will truly be complete. Acknowledging the full picture, you can then be at peace, even though each of you *does* go your separate ways.

There's an old Bible story that captures something of the truth that I am suggesting. It is the remarkable story set at Peniel, Seir, Succoth, and Shechem.

You will recall that Jacob and Esau had cohabited their mother's womb and had shared the nurture of the same home; yet after many childhood years together it became apparent that the two of them had embraced such radically different lifestyles—compounded by Esau's familial indifference and Jacob's outright deceitfulness, two elements that strain any relationship—that they could not continue living together in the same home. Indeed they parted as mortal enemies, with Esau clearly considering how to inflict fatal bodily injury upon his erstwhile companion. As you can see, this has many of the same components of a present-day divorce, not altogether unlike your own. That's what makes the resolution of their story such a powerful one for you to understand anew. You may read it in Genesis 32 and 33.

After years of separation, their inevitable moment of meeting occurred at a fording place in the Jabbok River, a place thereafter called Peniel, "the Reflection of God." We will return to the significance of what took place there.

By no means was it clear that this fraternal meeting would be an amicable one; for by this time, as someone has said, "many damns had gone over the water." Jacob confessed, "I fear him, lest he come and slay us all" (Genesis 32:11). A bargainer to the very end, Jacob laid out lavish presents as a gesture of appeasement, a desperate act of audacity and futility. Jacob must have recognized their true nature, for that night he is portrayed as a deeply troubled person, wrestling with an angel, a presence that has been variously interpreted as personal conscience, the Holy Spirit, or Jacob's unconscious self. It was an experience that literally marked his every step for the rest of his life. Yet in its awful moments, Jacob and God *both* laid hold of one another in such a profound fashion that the estranged Jacob would never again be the same person; he would be marked at a far deeper level than his dislocated thigh. And the deeper changes wrought by the wrestling are what I am hoping that you will find as you move through the dynamics of your own story.

On the next day, it became apparent that Jacob's gifts and gestures to his brother were totally unnecessary. For Esau was no longer the same person either! What an exciting, relieving, and ultimately releasing, discovery! In the long, intervening years, Esau had grown, too. An amazing grace had come into his spirit—yes, even to this one who had seemed so indifferent to the deeper issues of life. I hope that some of the basic themes of their story can eventually be played out in yours and J.'s story as well, so that you can both get on with your lives in health and hope.

Both parties of this long-ago "divorce" embraced in peace, kissed in affection, and wept with sweet sorrow/joy. Esau and Jacob were finally and truly at peace with each other, for now each saw the other through Peniel's looking glass of God. The divorce that had so grievously rent their generation in the covenant family was not cancelled, but it was concluded.

My hope is that the meaningful truth so obviously present in *that* story may be repeated in yours and J.'s story—*not* that your divorce will be cancelled; but that with the grace of God and your own growth, it will be concluded, releasing each of you to the possibilities of a healthy future, instead of leaving either of you bound to the should-have-beens of the past, or to the might-have-beens of the present.

This conclusion can happen, although it cannot be artificially rushed or manipulated. While some time needs to pass, your own conclusion need not take years to come about as it did for Esau and Jacob. Changes occur within each of us in the passing of time and because of separate experiences. In fact, you might find, to your surprise, that J. makes many positive changes, once the impediment of your presence has been removed!

Certainly Esau made changes. He "grew up" once Jacob was not around, seemingly inciting Esau's worst self. The person coming to meet Jacob was no longer the calloused, indifferent, blameworthy companion that the former family unit had known.

Still there was bound to be a certain tenseness in the meeting, as there is with some of yours and J.'s. Where does one begin? Who makes the first move? Here Esau, the more confident one, took the initiative of recognizing the changes that had taken place and the time that had passed. Thus he demonstrated forgiveness of the other, quite explicitly, in both word and deed. This was not a moment for ambivalent communication of the sort that divorcing people know so well. No ambiguous symbol. No implied gesture. No uninterpreted silence. Not on paper and not by proxy. But by a demonstrated word, the truth of which we Christians already know through our being the people of the demonstrated Word. Thus Esau "ran to meet him, and embraced him, and fell on his neck and kissed him, and they wept" (Genesis 33:4).

I don't expect that you and J. will reach your conclusion by amicably falling on each other's neck, but you can demonstrate the same meanings that are there in that long-ago scene as both of you reach some kind of closure, characterized by a demonstrated forgiveness at a real and personal level. Whether yours is an embittered schism or an emotional stalemate, in time one of you, and hopefully both of you, will understand that you have "grown up" from the person you were at the place of your parting, and one of you might risk the Esau role. Admittedly, that is a vulnerable role, especially if either of you assumes it too quickly. My hope is that one of you, or both of you, will recognize when such a demonstration of peace and wholeness is appropriate. Amazingly, countless couples like Esau and Jacob have testified that such a risky initiative works, when the time and conditions and parties have all matured. It works, even if neither person is "coming from the same place," as Jacob and Esau were not on that long-ago morning.

Some would probably have said that Esau was taking the role of a fool, for apparently right up to the end Jacob was still bargaining, dodging, scheming. Blatantly "pulling out all the stops," Jacob displayed his wives and children out front. He then went ahead of them, bowing himself to the ground seven times as he walked out to meet Esau. Even Jacob's bowing seems to be one more delaying tactic, as well as being an overplay of obeisance. Ignoring the gifts and the posturing, Esau went straight to the heart of the matter: he ran to meet Jacob, explaining, "I have enough, my brother" (Genesis 33:9). While it is not an accurate translation linguistically, I would like to stretch out the emotional reality of that moment and make it read, "*I have had enough.*" Certainly Esau was acting out that feeling. Using the same bit of linguistic license, we find—not surprisingly, I think—that part of Jacob's answer is to say, "I have (had) enough (too)." At least this is the way the story feels to me.

Eventually, I suspect one of you will realize that you are at such a moment, and you can say or do something similar. In God's providence there simply comes a time, not to get even, but to get through. It may be too early to do it right now, and that's all right. Someday. For Esau and Jacob it took years for their grace-full moment to occur at Peniel. While I am confident that the two of you could improve on their time-table, it would be hard to improve on the substance of their reconciled moment.

And we must not give all the credit to Esau. Something had happened to Jacob too, even though various parts of his lesser nature were still quite evident. We do not all grow at the same pace nor by the same pattern, and many imperfect people are aware of some marvelously transforming miracles at work in their still imperfect natures. That's part of the meaning of the Jabbok wrestling pit and Jacob's renaming of the site as a testimony to his having beheld a transforming God there.

Our modern highways eliminate the fording places of a simpler era, so to many of us this may be a foreign term. A fording place is an ingenious transition site, usually provided by nature without the machinations of humanity, where two different styles of life—land travel and water travel—cut dramatically across each other. With a little bit of forethought and caution, travelers going either way can proceed across the intersection in safety. Therefore, a ford is a good symbol for where the two of you will eventually find yourselves in your divorce travels.

A ford can be a frightening place, and if you are not careful it can be a dangerous place. Many land travelers slip off a fording place and are swept away to disaster; some water travelers have been known to run aground in the shallows of such a place; yet others find in the ford their own enabling possibilities to get on with the journey.

The "ford of the Jabbok" (Genesis 32:22) was a place of growing-up like Jacob had never seen before. Excited by his experience there, he wanted to rename it The-Place-Where-I-Have-Seen-God. Such an affirmation was tremendously different from the way most of Jacob's peers regarded such sites. Semitic society generally agreed that demons lived there, demons who were ready and able to do in the unsuspecting wayfarer who happened upon the place. Some people will assume that the same foreboding demons lurk within the landscape of your own divorce; but it need not be so, as Jacob joyfully came to understand. Instead of staring down the demonic, he found himself face to face with God, and he named the place for this new reality he had discovered. I believe that the time will come when you also will be able to testify to the presence, the touch, and the blessing of God at this transition place in your journey and J.'s.

In reality, then, both of these estranged figures from the patriarchal narratives of antiquity had been prepared by God to rise above their old selves. And it was so! A part of the reason why a story like this one becomes canonized Scripture is that subsequent generations discover a timeless quality about its theological and psychological truth, one which plays itself out again and again in human lives. I urge you, and J too for that matter, to think about your own story in relationship to this one.

But that's not the end of the story! Notice that there is a little denouement in the drama of that morning meeting at the ford, one that is sometimes overlooked, but which has a great deal to say to your and J.'s situation. In a tacit admission that it would not be possible for these grownup persons to live together, or even within sight of one another, the reconciled brothers parted: "Esau returned that day on his way to Seir. But Jacob journeyed to Succoth, and built himself a house, and made booths for his cattle" (Genesis 33:16, 17).

Graced with a presence beyond themselves, each had looked deeply with God at the other, acknowledging that neither was any more the long-ago enemy. Both now had some self-understanding and personal growth which they had not possessed previously, and both had at least some mature acceptance of who the other had now become. At this point they could truly go their separate ways in peace, with no lingering claims of unfinished business, either good or bad, upon each other. Peniel was the moment and place of recognition, but life has to go on somewhere else, in a reconciled but separate state, as symbolized by two entirely different destinations and habitations.

Unfortunately, some people succumb to the temptation to run off too quickly to their Seir or Succoth without properly allowing for the miracle of Peniel to take place. Some people in your situation spend too much energy and resources planning, and even writing, parts of their stories with other people in those eventual settings. Many can attest to the healthiness of not rushing this next part of the journey. They caution us against daydreaming away the strengths they are constantly discovering even in their present situation. I like that! No matter what, or who, either you or J. thinks you will discover at some Seir or Succoth, it is important right now to rejoice and to be glad in the present discoveries of the journey, without relying exclusively at this point on your dreams of the eventual destination. Why not allow your marriage to rest in peace, with both its failures and its successes acknowledged alike? In all likelihood you began it "in the presence of

God and these witnesses." Now, as you let it go, you are no less in the grateful presence of God and good friends. That's a blessing to be cherished, and rushing off to Succoth and Seir may obscure this truth.

If you read the story again, you will discover that Jacob made a point of saying that his own journey at this time had to be measured out at a definite pace, making allowance for the fact that as a responsible person he could no longer live only for his own satisfactions. "I will lead on slowly, according to the pace of the cattle which are before me and according to the pace of the children" (Genesis 33:14), was the way he put it. He also acknowledged that wherever and however Esau was going, the pace of the one was not necessarily the pace of the other, any more than were their destinations similar.

At your own individual pace, you and J. will go on separately, very aware that the God whom you have found anew at the "looking place" of Peniel keeps pace accordingly.

And what of your Succoth and Seir? Who knows? We only know for sure about the story of Jacob and Esau and how it came out. The Scripture tells us that Jacob built a house and some cattle booths at that new place. Those things imply settling in, adjusting to new surroundings, taking new people into one's circles of acquaintances. Nomads live in tents, and their animals graze on the open land, while permanent settlers build structures for themselves and their possessions. In these beginning weeks of your being a divorcing person you have constantly thought of yourself in "hang loose," nomadic terms; you are definitely unsettled. Some of that feeling is all right—in fact, some of it has probably been necessary for your sheer self-preservation. But divorcing processes do end. Eventually you will find yourself beyond your vulnerable, uncomfortable place and condition. There may indeed be some significant persons and possessions and settling-in experiences awaiting you and J. in some equivalent sites of Succoth and Seir. But, for the time being, the journey is your home, and our faith bears abundant witness that you have a Companion on the way. Rejoice and be glad in it!

There's even one more part of this amazing story, and it points you directly to the good news of Christ. After a sojourn in Succoth, we are told that "Jacob came safely [some translations read "in peace"] to the city of Shechem, which is in the land of Canaan . . . " (Genesis

33:18). And there he settled in as if he *really* meant business. Whatever he had done at Succoth, he did even more so as he claimed his future in Shechem. He carefully negotiated a purchase of real estate, and there he worshiped the God who never gave up on him.

Shechem has been an especially favorable site, for there was abundant water there, a key for survival. In fact, to this day there are guides at Shechem who will proudly show you "Jacob's well." His village and his well would return to center stage once again in the drama of grace many centuries later. And that story, too, has some helpful clues for your own growth.

In the fourth chapter of the Gospel of John we are told that Jesus came to this place. "Jacob's well was there, and so Jesus, wearied as he was with his journey, sat down beside the well" (John 4:6). While he sat there, the divorced Samaritan woman came and talked to him. In that conversation Jesus offered to her, in himself, that which he called "living water" (John 4:10).

The true peace and refreshment of your divorcing journey will come when you and J. and others like you find the same One. Years before, when Jacob came there in peace, he built an altar as a testimony of his faith in the God who had never given up on him. When Jesus came to the same place, his words about living water gave the same testimony, that God still never gives up on us—no, not even in the circumstances of divorce, as the Samaritan woman discovered that morning. You have only to open your heart to this same truth to sense the joy of his Presence.

As a divorcing person, you know what a sobering experience it is to let go of a love. As a divorcing person who learns some things along the journey, you can also know what a wonderful experience it is to find anew the Love that will not let *you* go!

To lose the earth you know, for greater knowing; to lose the life you have, for greater life; to leave the friends you loved, for greater loving; to find a land more kind than home, more large than earth——

—Whereon the pillars of this earth are founded, toward which the conscience of the world is tending—a wind is rising and the rivers flow. (You Can't Go Home Again, *Thomas Wolfe*)